A PLACE TO REMEMBER

Edited by

Natalie Nightingale

First published in Great Britain in 2001 by
POETRY NOW
Remus House,
Coltsfoot Drive,
Peterborough, PE2 9JX
Telephone (01733) 898101
Fax (01733) 313524

All Rights Reserved

Copyright Contributors 2001

HB ISBN 0 75432 708 6
SB ISBN 0 75432 709 4

FOREWORD

Although we are a nation of poets we are accused of not reading poetry, or buying poetry books. After many years of listening to the incessant gripes of poetry publishers, I can only assume that the books they publish, in general, are books that most people do not want to read.
Poetry should not be obscure, introverted, and as cryptic as a crossword puzzle: it is the poet's duty to reach out and embrace the world.
The world owes the poet nothing and we should not be expected to dig and delve into a rambling discourse searching for some inner meaning.
The reason we write poetry (and almost all of us do) is because we want to communicate: an ideal; an idea; or a specific feeling. Poetry is as essential in communication, as a letter; a radio; a telephone, and the main criterion for selecting the poems in this anthology is very simple: they communicate.

CONTENTS

Night Lights (Or Sleepless In Swansea)	Shirley R Thomas	1
Moonlight Over The Fells	Carolyn Smith	2
All This Beauty	Rosalind Wood & Martin Allen	3
Deafening The Children	Kim Montia	4
England - My England	Leonard T Coleman	5
Aware	Rodger Moir	6
Bank Holiday	Johanna Nicoll	7
The Scottish Parliament	J W Wright	8
Land Of Hope And Glory	Denise Shaw	9
Storm At Carrick	Marsha Durok	10
Teesdale Splendour	Frank Watson	11
English - And Proud Of It!	Denis Martindale	12
One Day At Dover Priory	Howard Thorn	13
Northumberland	Ellen Thompson	14
My Thoughts On Poppies	Noelle Hill	15
The Lost Glory	Margaret Gleeson Spanos	16
England's Country Ways	Rita Pedrick	17
I Cast My Eyes (About My Love Of Cornwall)	Nicholas Winn	18
The Lake District And Abroad	M E Smith	19
The Brecon Beacons	Norman Meadows	20
Cornish Colours	Les Merton	21
Time Warp (Milford-On-Sea)	Christina B Cox	22
Our Little Town	Barbara Davies	23
September In Canterbury	W Vidler	24
The Viewpoint (Glasgow)	Jillian Shields	25
York	Martin Snowden	26
The Graveyard's Story	G Wright	27
This England	F L Brain	28
Queen City	Vere Collins	29
Land Of Hope And Glory	Janet M Baird	30

A Serenade To The Valley Of Wye	Octavia Hornby	31
What A Thin Line	Stanley Swann	32
The Green Hills Of Somerset	Ailsa Keen	33
The Exile	Patricia Whittle	34
Devon In August	Karen Barron	35
M62	Julie Sennitt	36
Song Of September	Janine Vallor	37
Land Of Hope And Glory	Rita Cleary	38
Sea Road	Rajeev Bhargava	39
My Town	Margaret Stumpp	40
Millstone Morality	Jim Riley	41
A Change Of Heart	Eifion Thomas	42
Have You Not Been	W D Stanley	43
My Cotswolds	Martin Boyle	44
Two Domes Of Discovery	Joyce Ferguson	45
Exeter	Diana Price	46
Green And Pleasant Land	Andrew Brian Zipfell	47
Small Heaven (Bunhill Fields)	Juan Calle	48
Autumn	J Waterman	50
Memories Of Childhood	Diana Daley	51
The Promised Land	I R Cook	52
No Other Place	Helga Dharmpaul	53
The Dump	V M Archer	54
H(e)aven	Jamie Barnes	55
England's Heart	Savile Skyes	56
Drifting Smoke	Keith Coleman	57
A Winter's Day At The Frairs, Aylesford	Gill Sathyamoorthy	58
Land Of Hope	Patricia Evans	59
My Scottish Highland Home	Francis Joseph Lawton	60
Walsingham	Lorna Troop	61
This England!	Edith Antrobus	62
Sarum	Jonathan Stocker	63
Red, White And Blue	Audrey Allen	64
The Leper Chapel, Cambridge	Wendy R Thomas	65
The Exile	Joan Cooke	66
Freedom Town	Maxwell Anderson	67

Home At Last	Carole A Cleverdon	68
A Coastal Village	R D Harvey	70
A Devon Gem	Leo Taylor	71
No More Land	M Lawson	72
Bonnie Galloway	James Rodger	73
Narborough Trout Farm	Margaret Tungate	74
Haworth Moor	Angela Butler	75
Scillonian Days	Kath Hurley	76
Aberdeen - The Granite City	Christine Nuttall	77
Trevelyan Cottage, Allithwaite	Joan Todd	78
The Needles	Barrie Williams	79
The Surrey Day	Colin Skilton	80
Cornwall's Changing Scene	A Godman	82
Shamrock	Joan Boswell	83
Aldworth Giants	Graham K A Walker	84
Wales	Phyllis L Stark	85
Derwent Water At Dusk	Win Wilcock	86
Wouldham	Flo E Smith	87
Enchanting Places	Josephine Foreman	88
On Orchy Bridge	Michael Alan Fenton	89
Our Motherland	Kathleen M Hatton	90
Tranquillity	B J Eyre	91
The Moat	Roger J Gould	92
Where White Waters Flow	G J Von-Heizon	93
Rain On Argyle Street	Sarah Knox	94
Flatford	Andria Jane Cooke	95
Sidmouth Soliloquy	Rupert Smith	96
North Wales	Dennis Scott	97
The Homeward Call	Sharon Ferguson	98
Tally Ho!	D G W Garde	99
The 1st Of March	Marie Horridge	100
Spreading Chestnut Tree Evelith - Shropshire)	Ester Francisca Caruana	101
Co Down	Maggie Fairbrace	102
Holiday In Cornwall	Sheila Walters	103
My Sentimental Journey	Diana Frewin	104
Blakedean Moor	Kath Gabbitas	105
The Hampshire Down	Douglas Wood	106

Edinburgh - God's City	I H Davies	107
The Way To Emmanuel	Sheila Burnett	108
A Flickered Light	S Hamilton	110
Thoughts Of Long Ago	Sandra J Walker	111
Secrecy Of Bygone Days	F Gibson	112
Yorkshire Wonderland	Bernice Sharpe	113
Green Valley Grass	Catherine Craft	114
Holiday In Whitley Bay	Pauline Wilkins	115
This Timeless Land	J M Armstead	116
My Potted Plant	Dawna Mechelle	117
Canterbury	M A Challis	118
If They Returned (From The Past)	Walter Crooks	119
Memories Of England	Pete Simmons	120
The Silver Birch	Ann Copland	121
The Greatness Of Britain	H D Hensman	122
Seeing Rabbits From The Train	Sheila Jeffries	123
For Life	S P Springthorpe	124
Mayfield, Sussex	Katharine Holmström	125
Northumberland Landscape	Louise Rogers	126
Sussex, My Sussex	Ken Brown	127
St Edmund	Jonathan Covington	128
Land Of Hope And Glory?	Margaret Lightbody	129
Bread From Evans	Peter Davies	130
Slavanka	Louise White	131
Silent Spring	Anita Richards	132
Derry's Icy Tide	Perry McDaid	133
Autumn At Day's Lock	Carolyn Garwes	134
An English Delight	Albert Boddison	135
Old Ingestre	Dennis Marshall	136
Rainbow	Eve Devenish-Meares	137
The Kingdom Of Light (The Ardnamurchan Peninsula)	Shaan Everson	138
Sinners	Ray Ford	139
Schiller At Minack	Jacqueline Abendstern	140
Flora Orcadensis	J M Heddle	141
UK Sovereigns: A Brief History	Christopher Higgins	142
Vale Of Avalon	Dora Watkins	144

UK's Countryside Panorama	Hilary Jill Robson	145
Kernow	Elizabeth Morris	146
Summertime Splendour	Carol Olson	148
Monarchs And Princes Of		
The Third Millennium	E G Pryor	149
2001!	Barbara R Lockwood	150
On Reflection	Jack Pritchard	151
Third World Country	Ann Hathaway	152
The Millennium For The People	Dianne Brown	153
Looking On	Zoe Fitzjohn	154
Gate Of Life	Frederick Fordham	155
A Peaceful Time	Linda Beavis	156
Remembering	Elisabeth Dill Perrin	157
Daystar	Sandra Bond	158

Night Lights
(Or Sleepless In Swansea)

I love to watch the hill at night to see
The traffic that flows to and from the town.
There on the left side, rubies climb and glow -
And on the right, bright diamonds dazzle down.

The lampposts, tall and straight like sentries stand
And cast below their pools of amber light,
On cars and buses and on people too,
They are the silent guardians of the night.

Above, the stars - those lustrous lamps of heaven -
Sparkle and shine upon the scene below.
The moon, a slender silver arc, sails out
On seas of patterned clouds and indigo.

But all too soon arrives grey-fingered dawn,
I greet the morning with a sleepy yawn.

Shirley R Thomas

MOONLIGHT OVER THE FELLS

Dusk lies gently in the valley
Clothing silent fells in peace . . .
Eerie . . . the half-light of deepening sunset
Writes a new mystery play:
Bats and creatures of the night take their places
In another land,
Smoky curtains draw across fading fields,
Whisp'ring leaves and
Black waters watching with
Fathomless eyes . . .
Waiting to capture radiant stars
And grasp the lofty fells
As moonlight rises through
Ghostly, silver-tinged clouds
To bless the world
With a kiss,
A sparkling haze of
Diamond dew
Curling through the hedgerows and trees
In spectral forms beckoning
Skyward . . .
Moonlit figures of the night,
Yet, not of this world
They sweep the air
And scale the rising shadows
Of the crags
In the glorious pageant of
Moonlight over
The Fells . . .

Carolyn Smith

ALL THIS BEAUTY

The Romans named it Vectis
this wondrous 'Garden Isle'
Timeless in history
with its unique, tranquil style

Emerald green seas
Beaches of golden sand
Bays with secret caves
Lavish forests abound

Coloured cliffs adorn
Gentle waves caress the shore
So many hidden treasures
this island holds in store

As you look around
pause awhile for thought
Only here will you find
the calm and peace you've sought

This
Heavenly Place
Where all can just 'be'
'All this Beauty'
Is of God
Just for
You and Me

Rosalind Wood & Martin Allen

DEAFENING THE CHILDREN
(Intimidating the pupils of Holy Cross Primary School North Belfast - 6/9/01)

Blast bombs howling
Hatred casts its shadow on the day
Bigotry's infectiousness
Spreads rampant disarray

Horns and whistles sounding out
Their message on the morn
Another ray of hope
Is suffocated as it's born

Intimidation deafening
The children whilst they walk
Sinister the route to school
That terror chose to stalk

The ugly face of Loyalism
Peeps out from its mask
Sickening the world
As it sets about its task.

Kim Montia

ENGLAND - MY ENGLAND

England, the place where I was born.
Idyllic to my early childhood dream.
A place of winds and sunshine, clouds and rain.
Yet I would choose you home, if born again.

A simple place, uncomplicated plan,
Green fields and villages, where it all began.
Cox Orange apples, strawberries and cream,
A sluggish brown trout nosing-up a stream.

A brick-built schoolhouse, where I went to school,
Basic tuition village infant style,
To read and write, to add and multiply
Learning to live my life until I die.

That English-ness, so hard to quantify,
And yet desirable, that sense of right,
Framework for a life of Christian love,
A destiny that seems designed above.

The rule of Law to which we must ascribe,
The freedom to express our wildest dreams,
At risk of censure if we misbehave,
Our stern refusal to become a slave.

Through constant strivings, plagues, and even wars,
True to those principles, so bravely laid.
The tribulations of a savage Destiny.
By millions, gone before, to keep us free.

Leonard T Coleman

AWARE

I saw across a valley
Before she came to life
For deep below my feet
There's a force hard at work
Ready to put leaves upon each branch
Spring in the valley does lurk

For now I see clearly across
Still frozen in parts and bare
That river will flow again
When life begins anew
I'm aware of a sense of energy
As I stand to admire the view

The birds they talk among themselves
Sad frogs croak their songs
Shoots push through the soil
The ceremony has now begun
Spring with all its energy
Will replace all winter's done

And dear England will be alive again
Its pale valleys so cold and grim
The cuckoo robs another nest
The lamb will stagger at first
But gain strength from sweet milk
As the buds through the wood now burst.

Fields of England green
Roll until the end of time
Bless each grassy blade
Daisies are the proof
That life lives on in the ground
England will be saved

Rodger Moir

BANK HOLIDAY

Yet again, another Bank Holiday
What to do that was the question
A visit to the church to see
The Children's Flower Festival
So many clever ideas by them
And others a little older
While drinking tea, on offer,
Remembering times past
Other Bank Holidays with tea
At the vicarage
How we enjoyed that,
But time has moved on
It's no longer 1939
With a holiday in Yarmouth
On a lovely farm and where
During the night a storm erupted,
Followed three weeks later by Second World War
Memories, as I walked along the canal
With boats full of happy people
And over the Common taking in
All I had done and seen
On this Bank Holiday, now over.

Johanna Nicoll

THE SCOTTISH PARLIAMENT
(A proud and loyal citizen
(late of Edinburgh)
Octogenarian)

God bless our Scottish Parliament
Much happiness in all that they do
Gaining pride, honour and respect
Throughout the United Kingdom too

Scotland - one of four great nations
With England, Ireland and Wales
A proud and loyal union
Which never-ever fails
Great Britain - may it never be defiled
God bless our British Isles!

J W Wright

LAND OF HOPE AND GLORY

No glory in this land of hope
Just tears and sweat and fear that chokes.
Whatever happened along the way
That's brought us to our present day?

Land of hope was sung so proud
Now it's dead, it's in a shroud.
Buried deep, the glory's gone
Land of hope it has not won.

A steeplejack on high could hold
A belief in hope a desire so bold.
No one has the honour now
No pomp and splendour, no sacred cow.

So what has happened to this land
Where once dignity and praise held each other's hand,
Has homage died and lost respect?
Glory and hope in the land, a reject?

Bring the legacy, bring it back
Serve your term as a steeplejack.
So then we see a land of glory
And hope would tell another story.

Denise Shaw

STORM AT CARRICK

Walking softly over sand I look right out to sea,
Shudder watching storm approaching, time to run for me,
Finding tiny narrow cave, protected from the skies,
Once in, I turn to view the scene but can't believe my eyes,
Clouds rolling madly in the sky,
As growled the angry thunder,
Lightning tore throughout the Heavens,
And air was split asunder,
Burning, hissing, spewing rain was driving down to ground,
Plants flattened under tempest's rage, leaves muddied, tightly bound,
Sea lashed against the rocky shore, spray soaring, flying high,
Creating arch of silvered droplets, now here earth meets sky,
Wind rises further, howling now, round empty barren shore,
Propelling water into land, over rocks it tore.
Sand spirals upwards, changing form, becomes like solid wall,
Heaving, howling, twisting, trying not to split and fall,
Then quick as a flash the howling dies, wind's anger settles down,
Storm passes over nearby land, I take a look around,
Rocks were thrown in all directions, plants buried under sand,
Hard to recognise this place, now more like foreign land,
Beauty of the greatest kind, souls sweetly sugared balm,
I leave for home so pleased to know all is now quite calm.

Marsha Durok

TEESDALE SPLENDOUR

Come sit you down whilst I relate this tale
With regard to the wonders of lovely Teesdale.
No matter how far one travels, or what one sees.
There are few sights so spectacular as the River Tees.
One must climb high and walk far for its source to be found,
Where in majestic splendour it bursts forth from the ground.
Slowly and steadily it wends its course,
Its pace rapidly increasing as it nears High Force.
Now the roar of the water drowns even the Curlew's call,
As it thunders to the peak of England's greatest waterfall.
As it booms and crashes more than seventy feet
Its awesome splendour makes one's heart miss a beat.
Then it swirls around like a giant whirlpool,
Who would enter the water here? Why only a fool.
Many more wonders it reveals as it races rapidly on,
Many wondrous tales it could tell of times now long gone.
Now it flows on past villages, houses and farms,
Constantly revealing more and more magical charms
Then the river leaves the dale on its journey to the sea
And its message is clear, Teesdale is the place to be.

Frank Watson

ENGLISH - AND PROUD OF IT!

Blessed is the man of English birth where Christian kings have reigned
For heroes here have proved their worth! What legends we have gained!
Saint George is famous through the land, no craven coward soul,
He had a mission God had planned and bravely played his role!
Throughout the ages chivalry has signified us best,
We strive to act with dignity! In fact, we're quite obsessed!
Stiff upper lip and jutting jaw! We take life on the chin!
And when it comes to waging war, we'll fight and not give in!
We'll see things through, right to the end, till victory is ours,
Defending honour and each friend, opposing evil powers!
What courage runs in English blood! Britannia rules the waves!
We bring all challenges to God, by faith, for Jesus saves!
The world may change and planets too, yet England is our home,
It's at the heart of all we do and sweet as honeycomb.
The fields are green, the mountains gold with sapphire skies above,
Blessed is the land we daily hold within our hands with love.
What need have we for foreign soil? This England serves us well!
Blessed is the man defending loyal! On Earth! In Heaven! In Hell!

Denis Martindale

ONE DAY AT DOVER PRIORY

Sitting upon a seat here one late July day, an awareness of
cleanliness everywhere;
cliffs bearing their proud white shirt fronts, with variegated
crowns of green,
the Castle and its battlements denoting England's past, today's
proud heritage:
those fresh cream painted old architectural hotel fronts,
of character and elegance,
with harbour stretching in elliptical shape: broken in two by
a Lighthouse or two.
Sealink Ferries: they come and they go, akin to cars on today's
modern motorways,
a few small craft like chessmen: some big, some small
within the harbour walls;
a gentle rippling sea, signifying the calmness and serenity
of this day,
so time draws nigh, to bid farewell to this bright summer's day
at Dover Priory.

Howard Thorn

NORTHUMBERLAND

The land is bonny faced and fair
With all God's bounty gathered there,
Give me the voice to sing in praise
Of all her green and pleasant ways,
To paint the scene so vividly
That folk the world o'er long to see
Northumberland, my heart's delight,
From sandy shore to rocky height,
Each leafy vale and heather hill
Where crystal waters cowp and spill,
A-rippling through the verdant earth
Within these bounds that gave me birth.

Or maybe I should turn the page
Of history, our heritage,
From Viking horde to Norman knight
To many a bloody border fight,
Of coal that warmed a country's heart
And ships a-sail to foreign parts.

Far greater bards have played with words,
Heroic sons uplifted swords
For love of this dear land of mine,
Whose myriad virtues can entwine
The heart forever, holding fast,
In steadfast mould her folk are cast
Some journey far with no return
To this grand place where they were born,
No springing grass or cooling stream,
The hot sun burns and exiles dream
Of home on this beloved strand,
Northumberland, Northumberland.

Ellen Thompson

My Thoughts On Poppies

A tiny seed sown by the wind
Lies dormant till the time is ripe.
Friend of the plough, whose furrows deep
Awake the poppy from her sleep.

A symbol of our hope renewed,
Phoenix of the battlefield, struck by
Mortar bomb and exploding shell.
Many a gallant soldier fell.

In Flanders fields of golden corn
The scarlet poppy flowers erupt.
Today its crimson petals glow
A message of new hope they show.

We proudly wear the poppy flower,
Remembering their finest hour.

Noelle Hill

THE LOST GLORY

In my dreams they have dolled up the pleasure grounds,
something of its former glory.
Ten town houses with manicured lawns, with ample space for
many cars. Behind another lawn with tennis court and
kidney-shaped pool.
All this either side of the tree-lined avenue, where the red
chestnut grows.
The old ruin remains the same, clad in the ivy, with the circling
rooks and the odd old hooting owl.

I climbed the avenue gate, they shout at me to clear off,
get out of here.
I stand bewildered, saying I was born in that house pointing
to the old ruin.
Nobody listens to me,
On waking up, I am rather pleased, the old ruin and all its grounds
are still in dereliction and it's my brother's precious land.

Margaret Gleeson Spanos

ENGLAND'S COUNTRY WAYS

Dark alders frame the lazy river.
Insects drone among tall stems and leaves
Of yellow rocket flowers that quiver
Gently, in the summer breeze.

Land beyond, rise in patterned fold,
To greet the distant tree-topped hills.
Fields of corn reflecting gold,
Amongst the hedgerow, deeply filled.

Unspoilt countryside, warmed by the sun.
Laced with quiet twisting lane
And footpaths, leading one by one,
Through covered wood and open plain.

Watered by river and trickling stream,
Rippling by cool, and long.
Creating a land lush and green
Concealing life, birds and song.

The river meanders on and on,
And feeds the copious lake.
Filled with birds from home and beyond,
Here summer homes they make.

Oh! To be here in the summer's sheen,
Warm and lingering days.
To reflect upon this beautiful scene,
And of England's country ways.

Rita Pedrick

I Cast My Eyes (About My Love Of Cornwall)

From clifftop thrift and tormentil
Down craggy cliffs I cast my eyes,
To where Atlantic rollers spill
And surge beneath the seagull's cries:
Along the rocky shores and reaches
Where the yawning caves run deep
Where ships have broken on the beaches,
Where their gallant sailors sleep:

From tin mine engine houses tall
Where gorse lined pathways wind and twist
And granite canyons gape and fall
Beyond the bleak foreboding mist:
I cast my eyes above the ocean;
Watch its rhythm as it rolls
Forever in perpetual motion
Only God's good grace controls:

Old slate-roofed houses, beach bound streams
And ice cream, staring at the surf
Make Cornwall special in my dreams,
The cornerstone of English turf:
I cast my eyes beyond each crest
Frothing, foaming white, to roar
And pray that when I die, I rest
Forever on this Cornish shore.

Nicholas Winn

THE LAKE DISTRICT AND ABROAD
(A poem about quiet tranquillity)

Down from a sky of spangled blue -
From sequinned turquoise beam down -
Sunbeams philander with the dew -
Resplendent in a misty crown.
The spirit moves the soul of trees -
Who become with jewelled grace -
Mix with the flavour of the breeze -
Or flutter at his smooth embrace.
The stream caressing rocky cheeks
With laughter jingles!
To woo the sparkling shingles.

Behind the mist a mountain met a cloud -
So white, but soon she became black, she rained -
Or was she crying with a broken heart?
Mountain goats became afraid -
But the climbers pressed on regardless -
Through the storm there was no rest -
To reach the height of Everest.
The sun shone again, so the loving white cloud
Met her mountain again.

In spring the early flowers bloom, snowdrops appear
So welcome to see after the winter snow
Summer comes with the roses and leafy trees will be here.
But autumn comes along and sheds her leaves
Flowers will fade and wither then the winter snow again.
So we see the natural beauty is around us -
A product of God - the ecology of the Earth
So let us all enjoy it for all it is worth.

M E Smith

THE BRECON BEACONS

Climbing through Dowlais, past the lost miner,
past wives and children, hollow-eyed, hungry
forsaken, with every right to be angry;
but resigned to their fate on the back-burner.

Leaving coke ovens, black smoke: Pontypridd;
before me the mountains of Brecon beckon;
a green road twists upwards, like a bright ribbon
to sun-shadowed beacons and air I can breathe.

Subordinate time, geology king;
an ancient sculptor who with patient care
crafts hidden strata, forms hills stark and bare;
here the peewit's sad cry leaves my heart aching.

Hidden tarns in stone orbits that weep like eyes,
tranquil farmsteads nestling in deep valleys
contrasting with those smoke-darkened alleys
where hope always rises and never quite dies.

Thirsty and hungry I stop by a farm
told to expect I would not be welcome
as foreigners meet only with odium.
As if the traveller would come to such harm!

A man comes to meet me with impish elan,
greets me as if I were one of his clan.
'Thirsty now boyo? Have a drink; here, eat.
No charge, I'll say the sheep knocked the pail over.'
New bread and honey that smells of wild clover;
he smiles as I drink the milk, cow-warm and sweet.

This land of ours, of hopes and glories,
is so rich in history, fables and stories,
yet still I value beyond all others
the wealth of people who treat you as brothers.

Norman Meadows

CORNISH COLOURS

Gold is the colour of sand
that the sea can't wash away.

White is the colour of pyramids
built in the county of China clay.

Black is the colour of Bucca Du
the spirit blamed for disarray.

Gold is the colour of gorse
that brightens summer's day.

White is the colour of flying sea
that splashes rocks with spray.

Black is the colour of our flag
with its St Piran's cross inlay.

Gold is the colour that shines
when our rugby boys play.

White is the colour of blossom
decorating Cornwall in May.

Black is the colour of the Chough
that will bring Arthur home to stay.

Les Merton

TIME WARP (MILFORD-ON-SEA)

The unspoilt cliff walk is left to nature
Where wildlife nests in sandy craters
Yachts glide upon the ocean's breeze
Waves break from often troubled seas.

Dedicated benches line the high cliff path
Now others sit comfy on their laps
Enjoy fine views towards the Isle of Wight
Or just gaze into the sky at night.

No fish and chip shops line the front
No loud music or bungee jumps
There's no pleasure parks or noisy fairs
Just peace and quiet and good fresh air.

The village has a butcher's shop
Post Office and grocers in just the right spot
A bakers, chemists or a new hairdo
But when Wednesday comes they shut at two.

Yes, superstores have moved in near
But this village thrives that is quite clear
Restaurants, hotels, and holiday flats
Are around every corner with welcome mats.

Several pubs, it still can boast
With the friendliest of hosts
Good pub grub and best of beers
Are some reasons folks come here.

Mostly they come to retire
To live with simply peace of mind
Life is unhurried not a race
Before contemplating time and space.

Christina B Cox

OUR LITTLE TOWN

It was once a bustling little town, it's shop doors opened wide
Where folk who wore a happy smile would welcome you inside
A cosy little market selling pots of home-made jam
Laverbread and cockles, smells of freshly roasted ham.

Our spacious park, a hive of fun, a lively football game
A slide and swings, a spider's web, and a hefty climbing frame
Where the local youth would gather, each one to have their say
Each with a little tale to tell of the happenings of their day.

At the bottom of the High Street where the railway crossed the road
The busy old steam engine would pull its heavy load
And on the special holidays mothers' tightly held the hands
Of kids with spades and buckets on their way to Swansea sands.

Hear the tramping of an army of a thousand marching feet
Hob nailed boots on cobbled stones clink clanging through the street
As giant works of tin and steel calling workers to their job
Each body bathed in blistering sweat to earn an honest bob.

Gone alas these thriving times when a man could earn good pay
The ghostly works uprooted now, and carted right away
We have a pleasant cycle track where once the old works stood
Now men have time for leisure, and the exercise is good!

They're not there now, the busy stores that lined our teeming streets
Not many little cafe's where friends would love to meet
There is an air of sadness in our quiet little town
Where shops are closed, and shuttering in places bolted down.

A lively place, now laid to rest, has known a better day
But the progress of a prosperous world has watched it fade away
Now the old folk bask in glory on a solid plastic seat
To catch the strain of the ghostly tramp of a thousand marching feet.

Barbara Davies

SEPTEMBER IN CANTERBURY

Today the University
is surrounded by mist.

Poplars stand like blue ghosts.

Sun, gentle-fingered, filters through
to the city, where frustrated
traffic crawls.

      As I park
the car, attention's called
to ruby-red apples
clustered low, and hanging
temptingly reflected
in the waters of the Stour.

W Vidler

THE VIEWPOINT (GLASGOW)

The straight road, not that straight,
A small hill high, then down.
Towards cities who wait.
Their coloured lights ablaze,
Concealing sleeping life,
Through a misty, purpled haze.

I drive above the view,
My headlights make no mark
On the glimmering bright few.
The engine starts to slow,
As I remove the key.
The silence starts to flow.

The landscape, from these heights,
Is starred, and with slit eyes,
Seems to shine with Christmas lights.
As people sleep, it takes
Someone been here to know
Of the point that their house makes.

And make a point, it does,
For on this complex map
Is a glimpse of how man lives.
The sunset setting red,
Highlights each car's white lights,
People going or leaving bed.

This wondrous show goes on,
Silent movement of life,
Until the call of dawn.
Of the hope, I capture some,
As I leave to be a part
Of the view, for those to come.

Jillian Shields

YORK

If you've ever been to York,
and walked along the wall.
One thing you might have noticed,
is that people below, look small.

Looking in the distance,
which ever way you face.
You can see for miles,
but not from every place.

Someone's built some houses,
that block the scenic view.
This isn't very sensible;
it was a stupid thing to do.

When the wall was built,
there was nothing to block the vision.
It was built for observing;
approaching enemy, with a mission.

Martin Snowdon

THE GRAVEYARD'S STORY

An unknown warrior, in silent grace,
A guardian of time entombed in space,
Thrumpton's Village, history held in time,
Etched on stone in words sublime.

At the lonely church, atop the hill,
An empty grave we loathe to fill
No more to feel the rain and sun
But, to rest in peace life's story run.

From the ancient oak of countless years
The raindrops fall as silver tears
Amongst silent sentries carved in stone
All lain to rest, yet, not alone.

The poor man's soul, the squires too,
To the family grocer and me and you,
Over years long gone, they reached life's end
Before us, they too, to peace must send.

To that lonely church with mourning bell
And Thrumpton's graveyard with tales to tell,
Of warriors brave from times long gone
Who - with meekest souls - now lie as one.

G Wright

THIS ENGLAND

A tiny little island,
With a heart that's big and free.
Has seen many a conflict,
Boasts a chequered history.

We've often been invaded,
There's been many battles long.
We owe our very freedom,
To those who stood 'gainst wrong.

Once we had an empire,
Strong and very proud.
Independence they preferred,
To being in a crowd.

Today so much is changing,
That many have a fear.
Disaster once again will strike,
To a land they still hold dear.

The bulldog spirit lies hidden,
For dead it will never be.
It will rouse when the time arises,
To ever keep us free.

Yet we must remember one thing,
And many will agree.
We need to place our trust in God,
To keep our land GB.

F L Brain

QUEEN CITY

Fairest city of the West,
A spa beyond compare
Here is history manifest
With treasures rich and rare.
For 'twas to Bath the Romans came
When Aquae Sulis was its name.

In the Saxon abbey here
Was crowned the realm's first king;
Edgar changed the currency,
Defence encouraging.
And by the same illustrious son
Monastic revival was begun.

The legacy of Georgian times
Is with us to this day;
The circus and the crescents too
All rank in glad array.
Those ruined by an act of war
Now stand in glory as before.

So, Queen City of the West,
May tourists ever come;
To savour some of England's best
And take fond memories home.
For Bath's variety in Art
Creates a glow in every heart.

Vere Collins

LAND OF HOPE AND GLORY

Land of Hope and Glory,
A land of wartime story,
Don't ignore the old
For they have tales untold.
Listen to their words
Of far off harder days,
Open up your mind
Make sure you give them time.
For soon they will be dead,
Their words will be unread.

Janet M Baird

A Serenade To The Valley Of Wye

A beguiling serenade of beauty for the eye to behold
Fertile rolling meadows almost like a patchwork quilt
With their many colours of rich greens to golden browns
The forests of thick-leafed trees so high and so dense
Steep slopping banking dropping to a soft running brook
Then heading downstream to the fast flowing reaches
Where the waters leap towards rugged rocks and boulders
Till it makes an electrifying cascade as it tips over the weir
Descending furiously before continuing on its pathway
To calmer waters on the tranquil stream as it first began
While up above mountains tower in a pure majestic gesture
Inspiringly dappled with the streaks of heavenly sunshine
It is there where the peaks seem to virtually meet the sky
In a panoramic scene of impressive enthralling symmetry
Where the Earth seems to have stopped 'in a moment of time'
This wonderment of vision that can stir ones very heart
In this a halcyon serenade a dulcet melody of peace.

Octavia Hornby

WHAT A THIN LINE

How long do we pray for a world at peace?
And the silence when the hostilities cease
We must pray to our God what ever our creed
Sincerity is the key for this plan to succeed.

We need guidance from God to make it all last
The universal flag tied firmly to the mast
Religion is blamed for these earthbound sins
But as one war ends another begins.

Those surging masses of depraved humanity
Or should it read as downright insanity?
The anguish, all gone, their spirits are broken
UN gestures are but a mere token.

Some escape death by the skin of their teeth
Crossing the fields with mines underneath
These are the ones with luck on their side
As they shed their tears, and swallow their pride.

What of the homelands, they left behind?
Some of the future can be so unkind
What of the cultures and identity lost?
What of the future, what of the cost?

Stanley Swann

THE GREEN HILLS OF SOMERSET

Oh my heart is in the green hills of Somerset,
And no matter where my feet may roam,
Though they wander far and wide,
Over all the countryside,
In the hills my heart has made its home.

If you have never been down to Somerset,
I'm telling you, you don't know what you've missed,
The people there who meet you,
Smile with friendship as they greet you,
It's an atmosphere you simply can't resist.

In my dreams I see the green hills of Somerset,
And down in the valley see the lake,
Shining and serene,
Reflect the hillsides green,
And I wish I never had to wake.

For the sun paints the green slopes golden,
And the wind whispers softly through the trees,
The air is clover scented balm,
Everywhere is quiet and calm,
But for bird songs and the buzz of bees.

I wander down the winding lanes of Somerset,
Over low stone bridges crossing tinkling streams,
I find a village street,
With its houses small and neat,
And the hills are there in all my dreams.

All the beauty of our land is found in Somerset,
It's the place I'll always love the best,
Though I travel far and near,
There is nowhere quite so dear,
And it's there my heart will come to rest.

Ailsa Keen

THE EXILE

Oh England though you're far away
My heart is yearning much for thee.
I long to sit in solitude
Beneath an English apple tree.
Land of hope and glory, I miss you so
What bliss to walk where English flowers grow.
The memory of you ever stays
In dreams I walk your great highways
I think of dew upon the grass
O'er hills abounding mass on mass
The green, green land of patchwork quilt
The memories will never wilt
And though I grow infirm and old
Before I die that pot of gold
Within my heart and hands will hold.
When the flame of life can no longer burn
'Tis then to you I will return
To rest in peace no more to roam,
To England my beloved home.

Patricia Whittle

DEVON IN AUGUST

The hills were a surprise
then, as the week
and the sense of adventure progressed,
they became a sporadic shock,
the occasional 'A' road
lulling me into a false sense of space.
The dull mornings midweek
lulled me into a false sense of despondency
until I came to realise
that the sunshine is predictable.
The sea engulfed my senses
until I walked as though
a wave was constantly at my back,
swaying me to and fro with each step.
Children everywhere squealed with joy
at the unaccustomed pleasure
of sand, sea, ice cream and chips;
a combination only surpassed
by the thrill of doing it all again tomorrow.
And at the end of each day,
wine glass in hand,
I marvelled at the beauty of a crimson sky,
laced with the expectancy of another perfect day.

Karen Barron

M62

As I travel this country I may find
Many things which spring to mind,
But none so beautiful I seek
As the M62 where it's magnifique!

Between Leeds and Manchester did I drive,
Along the M62 just after 5.
My breath left my body, as I saw,
Hill upon hill, and then some more!

The roads were not safe with me around,
As I tried to keep my car on the ground.
I watched the hills more than the road,
Longing to be someone else's load.

The highest motorway in England, it may be
But you haven't lived until there you've been.

So what are you waiting for?
Go for a drive
Along the M62
Where the hills make you alive!

Julie Sennitt

SONG OF SEPTEMBER

Towards the hills of time I turn.
Mine, these loving days;
    full-bodied, September-ripened,
    mornings Mediterranean, warmed,
    hazed and soporific.

Time splendoured this summer's turning.

Hedgerows cobwebbed looped.
Dew-rose curl and furl sunned petals.
Grass blades ooze pearls
Air swirls of autumn wind
And mine, these loving days.

Furrows sepia-waved.
Swallows dart and part the honeyed winds.
Cider trees, apple bent;
Lemon scent of wild thyme,
And mine, these loving days.

Church spires Madonna'd blue.
Charcoal fires wisp and crisp the air.
Bees drowsy, nectar filled,
Harvests spill their colour lime,
And mine, these loving days.

Towards the hills of time I turn.
Mine, these loving days;
    September full, ripe-bodied,
    mornings michaelmas, warmed,
    hazed and soporific.

Time splendoured this summer's turning,
and scythed my days
        but, burning gold.

Janine Vallor

LAND OF HOPE AND GLORY

Fond memories abound
Of my first maiden trip to Thoor Ballylee, Gort Go Galway
Where the renowned poet WB Yeats
Spent many fruitful years of his life
I visualise him writing copiously
Beneath adequate or inadequate lighting in those days
How his head pounded out those riveting sentences and ideologies
They were so pregnant with wisdom and renown
I often wondered about his meeting with various dignitaries
I am sure they all brought the rafters down . . .
With their gay repartee
The renderings of verse and plays
Would indeed have heightened the ego
On entering Thoor Ballylee Tower
One reminiscences of visiting an old coach house or forge
The walls are covered in ivy
A stream flows gently along by the back
It gushes so much peace and calm
Indeed a haven for any sage or scholar
As you wind your way through the portals
A great store of literature and memorabilia
Echo forth the greatness and richness
Of such a wonderful poet
His imagination must have been fired continuously
With this little bit of Heaven upon Earth
The plumage of the Wild Swans at Coole
Did bring victory far and near . . .

Rita Cleary

SEA ROAD

The place to be, for me, is Margate's Sea Road,
where the sea and sky seem merged,
in light shades of delicate blue,
and cold dignified winds blow strong.
And waves of cold water whoosh and mix in with sand.

Rajeev Bhargava

My Town

We live in a beautiful place
In Wales not too far from the Snowdonia Range
On a nice clear day Snowdonia peak we see
And the smoke from the train winding its way to the top
Where fantastic views, when it's clear, you can see.
There is a castle in Harlech, the town where I live
With mountains, and miles of sea and sand
A safe beach, where children can play and swim
From the top of the castle wall you can see.
Beautiful scenery from all around
There are also slate caverns not too far away
Where you can go down in wagons to the depth below
Where slate blocks were mined and brought above ground
And split to make roof slates for the houses around
Now they are all silent, but one mine works on
Quite an experience to see how they worked
In the damp, and the dark, but a torch, underground.

Margaret Stumpp

MILLSTONE MORALITY

The millstone of democracy hangs heavy round my neck
It suffocates my conscience though it's something I protect,
The liberal democracy, the value of the vote,
By the people, for the people, sticking in my throat,

I loved you and I trusted you and still you let me down,
Seduced you are by capital and men in blue and brown,
In these dark days I should attack, there's not much to defend,
But the morals of a liberal stifle means to reach the end.

Jim Riley

A Change Of Heart

In the middle of the mid Wales valleys,
Just my luck to break down here,
Literally in the middle of nowhere,
Not a living soul anywhere near.

Nothing but enormous mountains
Baring down upon me,
Dominating the entire landscape
For as far as the eye can see.

Clouds perch themselves on the hilltops
The whole area untouched my man
Standing here makes me realise
Just how small I am.

The winds race through the valleys
The force of it takes me by surprise
My whole body is full of its energy
When suddenly the winds force dies.

I think to myself 'What a wonderful place'
My eyes shed a single tear
I've never felt this way before
Just my luck to break down here.

Eifion Thomas

HAVE YOU NOT BEEN

Have you not been to Blackpool?
Have you not walked the golden mile?
Have you not been bed and breakfast?
Have you not seen a landlady smile?

Rode on the front in November at night?
Seen illuminations light a little child's face?
With colour and glitz in its splendour
So bright can be seen out in space.

Taken a tram ride to Bispham?
And all the way back just for fun?
Then spent all your change in the arcades?
Holding cuddly toys you have won?

For a show gone to the Winter Gardens?
Got your ticket and waited in line?
Then sat in your seat with toffees and crisps?
To see Ken Dodd for the seventeenth time.

Have you not stopped to purchase some rock?
For relatives staying back home?
And while walking give in to temptation
In an hour or so it's all gone?

Have you not been up the tower?
Have you not been on a pier?
Have you not been for a ride on the donkeys?
Or had fish and chips with your beer?

Have you not joined all the thousands?
On deck chairs sat in the rain?
With cones of dripping ice cream
Saying eh! We must come to Blackpool again.

W D Stanley

My Cotswolds

Cotswolds, my Cotswolds
So near and so green
As I move slowly through you
Where have I been?

Your slopes roll gently
With thickets and meadows
Where livestock graze slowly
Between the hedgerows.

Sometimes densely wooded
You stand there so bold
But your softness and magic
Are there to behold.

Dwarfed in the folds of your generous embrace
Alone stands a cottage of yellow-grey stone
And a church and houses clustered together
To be here with you, is to come home.

Oh how I'm filled with peace and joy
To me you are a friend who stays
You are my strength, my hope, my dreams
Your comfort and charm; enchanting always.

Martin Boyle

TWO DOMES OF DISCOVERY

A dome was built in fifty-one to show innovations to everyone.
The people came from far and wide to view the miracles inside:
the inventive worlds of television, mechanical and electrical precision;
to show the Britons, weary from war, they had a future, bright not poor;
a world where they would have a place, and life would
                                           sport a happier face.

New journeys of discovery, brought home some new technology:
computers entered every home, and through the web the people roamed.
Mobile phones in every hand, masts and cables marched the land.

A dome was built in millennium year, but too few people did appear.
It showed the people how far they'd come from the miracles
                                                  of fifty-one.
But television already revealed both future and historic world.
Saturated with all things new, no need for them to visit, too.

Two worlds, fifty years between. Wonders experienced, marvels seen.
So much on which to think and chew, our world has
                                        widened; narrowed too.
The British have come far since then, that world our
                                        ancestors would ken;
our land internationally endowed, a global village we live in now.

Joyce Ferguson

EXETER

Incomparable and fair
Old when the Romans came . . .
And gave the city its famous name
Exeter's my city, the city of my heart.

Oft have I left it, only to return
With deeper attachment than ever.
For who brought up in this place
Would change for any other.

Bathed in the rosy light of the setting sun
What other city can be seen close by
From a cornfield.
Shining estuary to the left,
Far to the west the blue hills and tors of Dartmoor.
And nestling between,
Amid the soft green hills, Exeter.
The honey-coloured walls of the Cathedral
Turn rose-red at sunset.
Bathing the city in a golden glow.

Today there are noisy, polluting mini-buses, traffic jams,
And the odd crime or two.
But Exeter's pulsating heart never changes
Only beats with the times,
And stays ever faithful
To those who know her best
Giving a richer depth of living
Than many a smaller town or greater city.

Diana Price

GREEN AND PLEASANT LAND

As I look at this green and pleasant land,
Forests are gone, in their place buildings stand,
Farms are just ruins, their livestock gone,
The earth bare and barren,
    until developers come along.

In one single corner, of what was once a green and pleasant land,
Stands one single wood,
Untouched by man's hand,
Filled with blossoms of wild flowers that still grow,
The strong scent of the pine,
    is carried in the wind as it blows.

Every time I gaze upon it, my heart fills with woe,
I wonder realistically how long it will be allowed to grow,
After man discovers it and deals its mighty blow,
When he brings in developers to reap but not sow.

Yet in my heart, they will never take from me, the memories I have.
Of this special place I see,
For in my heart as I gaze with open hand,
I know this is mine,
My green and pleasant land.

Andrew Brian Zipfell

SMALL HEAVEN (BUNHILL FIELDS)

Bed of immortal sages,
Stones carved in pain,
Flowers of mythic colours,
Fountain of wisdom in
The air.
Yesterday is full of
Your art, knowledge and science:
Hundreds of years!
Some of them, spent in the valleys,
Others by the river
Where the light of reason shine
In a small cup of love,
Where the stories are born
And kings and princesses awake
To conquer the naïve heart,
The melody of the Innocent
Child and
The fly of the eagle
That gazes upon the aura in
Waters of pure gold.

There repose immaculate:
Milton, Blake and Bunyan
All in graves of mighty to
Fill the earth with wonder.

And I feel strange and dizzy
Walking in-between ghosts
Now turned angels,
They still tell stories
Straight from the fountain of glory
And they smile at my shadow
And smell
The perfume of the roses on my hand.

I'd like to be an echo
And sing your songs of love,
For this place is a palace,
A small heaven full of stars,
They glow and shine
Day and night
And swim at one
Forever with delight . . .

Juan Calle

Autumn

The rising wind moans outside,
and gains in strength with the turn of the time.

It rattles the slates as it circles the house,
covering the noise of a scurrying mouse.

The flickering lights finally dim,
so only the fire illuminates within.

As the wind reaches its noisy height,
driving rain arrives with the night.

And then the squall dies away,
as evening leaves with its final rays.

The farm that stands alone on the hill,
is safe inside from the evening's chill.

All returns to peace and calm,
as the clouds depart the hill side farm.

J Waterman

MEMORIES OF CHILDHOOD

As I was sitting alone in the park
I found my mind wandering into the past
Recalling favourite places and happy times
Paddling in the river Nene at Stanground
And trying to learn how to swim
Not succeeding but having fun
One winter, skating and sliding on the ice
When the fields had flooded over from the river
Taking a jam jar and catching tiddlers
Or chasing butterflies with a net.
The river branched off from the Nene at Peterborough
And we often walked across the fields into the city
Learning to ride a bicycle on the road outside
Mona let go of the seat and I was on my own
Going down hill with a bend at the bottom
Not knowing how to steer or stop, I just jumped off
But soon I had mastered the art of cycling
Then playing hopscotch, skipping and hide and seek
Flying home-made kites in the sky
Then going home to Mum's Victoria plum jam and crusty bread
Oh, happy, happy days at Stanground,
But all too soon they were at an end
For we moved when I was eleven
And with homework and household chores to do,
For me childhood was over.

Diana Daley

THE PROMISED LAND

Come with me and take my hand
I will take you to the promised land . . .
Heaven is the place we will be welcome there.
So much love and comfort to share.
We will stay together until the end our hearts will
Bind together just like friends . . .

I R Cook

NO OTHER PLACE

Beautiful Highlands, in verses and song
For centuries man has sung your praise.
These words are endless and shall remain long
After we have gone, and others will raise
Their glasses high to honour you
With a wee drum of your elixir of life.
Oh Highlands of Scotland with your lochs so blue,
Where ancient legends still survive.
Wherever else I may have been,
Or still may come to be,
No other place can ever mean
As much as you to me.

Helga Dharmpaul

THE DUMP

'Don't go to the dump!' my mother would say.
But that was where we most loved to play!
Of course it was dangerous - a river ran there
And broken glass shards were strewn everywhere,
Rusty, wrecked bicycles, smelly tin cans,
Useless chairs, sofas, pots and pans.

There was also a carpet, a lovely one!
At home we'd only linoleum
With coconut matting, so hard to bare feet,
While the grass at the dump grew lush and sweet.
We all lived in gardenless terraces
So here was the only grass there was.

Ugliness reigned in our end of town
For in many streets the bombs had come down.
While we hungered for beauty and spent happy hours
Feasting our eyes on the commonest flowers
And breathing their freshness, angels kept
Watch o'er this bank where Titania might have slept.

We had not much of this world's wealth
But were rich in laughter and rich in health
And here many fortunes we would amass
From the fairy purses in the grass.
If a rainbow perchance did over us bend
We would search for gold at the rainbow's end.

We looked in the clover four-leafed ones to find
And fed upon vetch of the purple kind,
If stung by a nettle, nearby was a dock
And a dandelion provided a clock.
Then decked out in daisy chains home we would romp
After our happy play at the dump.

V M Archer

H(E)AVEN

Have you ever been to a place, so clean, crisp and clear.
It is a wondrous site to see, open your heart and shed a tear.

It's a place with love and songs and dance, happy faces
smile as they pass by.
If you didn't know, it could be heaven, it's where the
ocean meets the sky.

Fame and fortune await, good value and quality food.
Smile on your face or your money back, just to keep you in the mood.

Romantic, memorable, meaningful, with your love if you want to kiss,
The place where Royalty lives, is down in Bognor Regis.

Jamie Barnes

ENGLAND'S HEART

Where lies the heart of England now, in this tumultuous day?
Not seen on screens that momently a darker land portray.
Above the traffic-growl of streets there's few can hear the beat,
To siren's scream in ghetto hell, life's message is defeat.
The simple truth of who we are, the oneness once we shared -
With values mocked, our saga scorned - seems lost and Hope despaired.
The heart of England withered - but break it never will.
It abideth everlasting, and you can find it still.

In a garden drowsy with lavender scent, where English roses blow,
In an orchard crowned with blossoms, soft-falling white as snow.
It's the smell of new-mown lawns in softly falling rain,
The sight of peeping primroses beside a Saxon lane.
Where swallows nest in chimney nooks and honeysuckles cling,
And robin, lark and speckled thrush their silver sonnets sing.
Where lofty oaks through centuries watch lifetimes spring and fade,
And resting flocks with bleating lambs from summer-heat seek shade.

In the ancient church that slumbers beneath the boughs of yew,
'Cross the churchyard green at daybreak, when the sward
                                        is thick with dew.
Hanging limp above the choir stalls with guardian angels nigh,
To glory long-forgotten, where hopes uncertain fly,
A simple cross of red upon a field of white,
That whispers, 'O fair England,' but does not speak of might.
Where English tongues sing hymns of joy, so those that hear
To England's heart uplifted, can draw near.

Savile Skyes

DRIFTING SMOKE

The smoke curls upwards from the gardener's fire
Drifting slightly on the evening air
White wisps creeping into the autumn sky
Fallen leaves from the trees now bare.

Upon the fire the gardener heaps
The obsolete pea sticks their task done
Feed the fire and to a cinder burn
The sticks that in the spring young tendrils clung.

Pruned clippings from the fragrant rose
The ever hungry fire spits and pops
Flames lick and dance a merry reel
A barrow load of potato tops.

Twigs and branches from off the bush
Weeds a plenty piled up high
Rotten apples, seed packets crumpled
The smoke drifting ever to the sky.

The garden now all tidy and neat
On the fire all the rubbish and trash
Into the night red embers glow
Come morning, just a pile of ash.

Keith Coleman

A Winter's Day At The Friars, Aylesford

In-between the wind and rain and ice
dawns a day of clear blue skies.
A perfect backdrop for the grey stone walls of Aylesford.
The winter's weak sunlight filters through bare branches
And touches ripples on the lake with light.

Swans are first to greet the lone visitors
Ruffling their shiny black feathers in style,
Ducks waddle over to add their voice
And gaggling geese run across the lawn to join the throng.
A host of birds wait expectantly for handouts
They shout and call but all to avail
for the visitors come empty-handed to the lake.

The Rosary Way's ceramics all locked up for the winter
Only the gardeners are working away
pruning shrubs and digging out old stock.
A fire crackles and spits devouring the rubbish and wood
Smoke drifts upwards till caught by the wind
is dispelled in the cold winter's air.

Few pilgrims here today to walk the Rosary Way
And see the pathway patterned by pressed damp leaves
And scattered twigs from broken branches
Or the diamond-like lights on the Medway River
dazzling the eyes so bright
that the river turns red around the edges.

Prayers in the chapel, silent or unsaid
Thoughts and aspirations dimmed,
The darkness coming from within
is touched by the diamonds in the river,
God's light in the world seen as His Son.

Gill Sathyamoorthy

LAND OF HOPE

Hope to have a decent school, can't grow up to be a fool,
Hope to get a job that's right and qualify without a fight.
Hopefully can make a plan to work and save in this old land.
Full of hope the British are, most of them will not go far,
It's still a land of class and riches, hope for others? In the ditches.
Paying taxes far too high, fuel charges reach the sky.
Hope to help the very poor, if they can't pay, then out the door.
Living in these unfair Isles we are hoping all the while.
Hope to not get sick today, money talks, so doctors say,
Hope the NHS get by, run it down and people die.
Hopefully to die in peace, hope by then all worries cease,
Wish I found life to be fair, hope my loved ones say a prayer.
Hope is in my will to find, hope is all I left behind,
St Peter's Gates are now ajar, all hope gone, now I'm a star!

Patricia Evans

My Scottish Highland Home

Bonnie blooms the heather on those Scottish hills of mine
The sun has casts its rays, and the morning mists have gone
The darkened glens grow lighter as the sunshine freely moves
And the native birds they twitter while they drink the honeydews.

When I leave my homeland it stays within my heart
No matter what the time may be for I am thinking of my home
I take with greatest pleasure the sight of Scottish heather
And make myself a promise no more that I should roam.

For myself with no ambition to change my ways in life
As long as I can gaze upon my Scottish highland sights
No man could want better than to breathe the sweetest air
There is not another place on earth that many can compare.

I have been so happy all these years but surely I must die
And among my Scottish highlands my body it shall lay
I will be there for all time at peace I will surely be
In my little Scottish heaven that was home sweet home for me.

Francis Joseph Lawton

WALSINGHAM

W ithin a village, time stands still and dreams
A way 940 years. Annunciation's vision
L ures all. Kings, queens and humble folk
S ide by side, barefoot along a holy mile.
I magine, on a sacred site, in Edward the Confessor's reign,
N azareth's House in replica, created by Richeldis,
G raceful, Lady of the Manor. Her inspiration
H eavenly, equalling Jerusalem, Rome and Compostella,
A wakening prayer, obedience, fidelity to God's commands.
M ary's love transcends time, embraces thousands, once again.

Lorna Troop

THIS ENGLAND!

People always grumble,
Folks just love to natter,
But this should always be about,
The things that really matter.
People have opinions,
Politicians like to bicker,
Everyone tries to rush around
To try and get there quicker.
Some people like to emigrate,
To get another life,
But find some things are not so good,
They have their struggle and strife.
We find most people just stay put,
They don't ever want to roam,
They want to stay in England,
Because England is their home.
Home, is where the heart is,
Is quite a well known phrase,
And really happy family life
Would make it a better place.
Here is where I want to be,
In England's pleasant land,
I've planted my feet firmly
And here is where I'll stand.

Edith Antrobus

SARUM
(Salisbury Cathedral, 31st May 2000)

Leaning spire with your windmill point,
Reaching up from your gravel bed.
We repair, your stone re-anoint,
Your figured frontage time eroded.

Faith keeps you anchored to the earth,
Carved so monumentally,
Firmly fixed, but a floating berth
In a cosmic totality.

Viewing closely, we here inspect
Renewal and unageing intellect.

Oasis of spiritual solace and calm
Where thousands flock for healing balm.
As clouds form in the blue beyond,
Water rushes from ancient mill pond.

All invade your green meadow land
Where serenely, you look on and
Protect your see as centuries pass;
Pastoral peace flows through reed and grass.

Jonathan Stocker

RED, WHITE AND BLUE

When I'm away from these
shores, I dream of you.
Wrapped up, in Red, White and Blue.
I think of long country lanes,
with a stream running by,
and a bridge to the other side.
Then across the meadows,
now knee high, in green waving
grass, to a secret place,
I knew as a girl.
I sit and think of
London Bridge, Westminster near by,
a poet's dream, and I am so
proud of Shakespeare, knowing he is ours.
Yes, I'm proud to be British.
And I fly the flag wherever I go.

Audrey Allen

THE LEPER CHAPEL, CAMBRIDGE

I gaze upon the aged walls
And see the faith behind
Weak and tired, crippled bodies,
Where God gave peace of mind.

I hear the anxious plaintive cries
Of those heads bent in prayer.
I hear God's voice, as He replies
That He, does really, care.

I hear those singing hymns and psalms,
Offered to Him, on high.
They knew, deep down, within their souls,
That death they would defy.

Although I sense profound despair,
I do not feel sorrow,
As those that closed their eyes from us
Woke in God's tomorrow.

And so, an air of calm prevails,
Echoing from the walls.
The faith of those that worshipped here,
Forever, boldly calls.

Wendy R Thomas

THE EXILE

For just the smell of autumn nights in England
Of lilacs bloom, of seaweed on the shore
The sight of summer skies and sunny mornings
My mother's face, the ivy round the door

And just to gaze on hills in dreamy Devon,
The river's mist and oh for just the sight
Of England's shores, I give my heart, my lifetime
For all these things, my heart cries in the night

The long damp grass on peaceful sunny mornings
The sweet glad smiles of all the folk I know
I pray I'll soon return to dear old England
To all these things I love, I miss them so.

Joan Cooke

FREEDOM TOWN

Freedom a song we seldom sing
Freedom a word that's used and abused
Freedom a chant, a song or a verse
Freedom's a man we owe a thanks
Freedom's a room in an empty house
Men have fought and died in its name
Freedom a place we all once knew
Freedom a river when it reaches the sea.

Maxwell Anderson

HOME AT LAST

A sail in the sound
Skimming the waves
Light breeze that blows
Surrounding all boats
Sending up horses atop of the waves
Look out, the breakwater's near.

Plymouth Sound in the sun
What a picture, seen from the Hoe
Crystal sea water, sun sending up stars
Pure white horses riding the waves
This gateway to freedom
For sail boat and sub.

I would sit and I'd watch
Vessel's out on the Sound
Warship sailing in on the tide
Then out on manoeuvres, to check out the seas
Who knows next week it could be the Med
There is romance in tales of the sea.

Early morning, sea mist rising
Just a hint of the wonders to come
Soft mist on your hair, light breeze is the wind
Smell of salt water, that grabs at the soul
Once you are caught your love will not die
This love of the sea with you until time.

No matter where I go
England, Scotland or Wales
I will always find myself
Back to the sea, why did I leave?
Now it's too late, I've gone too far away
But one day we will meet again.

Then it will be for always
No more will I roam
Scattered in the Sound
Watched over by the Hoe
Safe, at last my home
Plymouth Sound.

Carole A Cleverdon

A COASTAL VILLAGE

A shanty town with rutted tracks
Pretending to be roads,
And garden gnomes beside the shacks,
Plaster geese and plastic toads.

Here and there a prefab peeps
And winks at the mobile homes.
Across the lawn a white cat creeps
Between the painted gnomes.

Is it real or is it a dream:
The railway carriage dwellings,
The close-cut lawns and arbours green,
With secrets they're not telling?

Is anything real in shanty town?
Behind the prefabs rise the dunes,
Beyond the sea's grey billows frown,
And mermaids sing their echoing tunes.

Reality comes all too soon,
The waves crash on the shore,
Winds howl amid the gathering gloom
And wild the breakers roar.

Trellises shake in the raging blast
And gnomes tip sideways into ponds;
Prefabs shake and folk stand aghast,
As darkness and chaos rules.

Fearful they stare at the boiling sea,
The surging breakers tossing their spray . . .
Toy windmills turn their sails with glee,
Wishing wells float to greet the new day.

Then silence creeps stealthy round staunch-standing shacks,
And the white cat preens amid seaweed-strewn tracks.

R D Harvey

A Devon Gem

Sidmouth!
One of the last refuges
Of ladies and gentlemen;
People from a forgotten world
Despised and castigated
By our generation!
Would that our nation
Could learn some lessons
From its old world gentility;
Would that we had the humility
To salute the preservation
Of standards once held dear!
Leisure and recreation
Is enjoyed within its environs
With good fellowship, not violence:
A remembrance of the past
Which could light the way
To many happier years.

Leo Taylor

No More Land

This is a small town fourteen miles from Perth,
People came from towns near and far,
Our rural atmosphere to absorb every year,
Holiday ending homeward bound with new vigour.

They returned to the cities of their birth,
Having savoured tranquillity of country life,
Their life regenerated for another year,
Until returning for a peaceful holiday.

Country pursuits were followed with great zest,
The golf, the fishing and the walking too,
In the evenings, if so desired,
Dancing was the pleasure so aspired.

Long since have those days passed away,
Gone are the fields, houses instead,
Where cattle grazed beside the sheep,
The serenity has since gone astray.

Not many go fishing, no catch!
The golf is for tourists only.
For locals it is not affordable,
The parks have their toilets removed.

Who in their right mind would go there?
Parks without facilities are no use,
Ask anyone who has children,
They cannot be left to their own device.

There are no green belt areas,
All being built upon, no country life left,
Where is the glory in building,
On every space of earth in sight?
At the end of the day, what is there left?
Certainly no land, glory to expand.

M Lawson

BONNIE GALLOWAY

Peace on earth and goodwill to all men
Surely that sums up the place of my birth
Wigtown, in Dumfries and Galloway
This tranquil, sleepy little town
Which is beginning to stir a little
After being made Scotland's book town
Here I was born and here I hope to die
Like my father and his father before him
Here at least I feel free
Of the crowds and bustle of cities
The slower pace of the country suits me to a tee
One day in a city is enough for me
Wigtown Bay and Wigtownshire tells you
Of the importance of this place in days gone by
Now outgrown by Newton Stewart and Stranraer
Once a bustling port, now a favourite walk
By the River Bladnoch, you can take your ease
Or have a picnic under the trees
Ten miles down the road is Whithorn
The cradle of Christianity in Scotland
Wigtown has its martyr's drowned at the stake
Many people come here to retire from over the border
And share in the Galloway Hills, if climbing is their scene
Not quite Munroes but formidable just the same
Although mostly in the Stewartry the other half of Galloway
(Kircudbrightshire) shelter for Robert the Bruce
In his struggles for freedom, where he was reputed
To have watched the spider try try again
This was his land of hope and glory
As it is mine to the end of my days.

James Rodger

NARBOROUGH TROUT FARM

A day at the trout lakes
So calm and serene
A few muddy patches
Where anglers have been

A haven for wildlife
There's plenty about
And if we are lucky
We may catch a trout.

There's rabbits and moorhen
And wild geese and duck
Oh yes/he has caught one
I thought we'd have luck.

Relaxed and happy
Some fish in the bag
We've eaten our pack up
And John's had a fag

A few hours sport
And homeward we go
We've caught quite a few
You'll be pleased to know.

Some tasty fish dinners
We savour with pleasure
And think of the day
We spent fishing at leisure.

Margaret Tungate

HAWORTH MOOR

Too many wild Decembers
have ravaged farmstead timbers
dislodged the roof, once in tact
and turned our fantasy to fact.

Devotees of Wuthering Heights
those that search for literary sites
flock to climb Top Withins' hill
and feel the Heathcliff magic still.

Minute books of Gondal Tales
locks of hair, low picture rails
nursery samplers, Charlotte's shawl
and Branwell's scribblings on the wall.

Parsonage then, museum now
treasured objects showing how
time and place dictated life
and bred a secret world of strife.

Brontë charm and history
breathe enduring mystery
inspiration for their verse
and centre of their universe.

Rock and heather, waterfall
biting wind and curlew's call
Emily found her freedom there
however bleak, however bare.

If you ever hear the lark
on Haworth Moor growing dark
recollect her liberty
in nature's diverse harmony.

Angela Butler

SCILLONIAN DAYS

Splashing sounds of waves on sand,
Sun on bodies getting tanned,
Shrieking children running free,
Mean Scillonian days for me.

Screaming gulls with plaintive cry,
Helicopters droning by,
Small craft bobbing in the bay,
Trippers over for the day.

Perfume of 'Three Cornered Leek'
Seaweed smell and diesel reek,
Ornithologists galore
Racing round a rocky shore.

Island-hopping every year
In 'Sea-King' or in 'Buccaneer',
Tresco, Bryher, Martins, Gugh,
Samson and St Agnes too.

Relaxed and lazy sun-filled days,
In so many different way,
Scilly Isles you call to me
Far off across the Cornish sea.

Kath Hurley

ABERDEEN - THE GRANITE CITY

Glistening Granite City
Your buildings tower by the sea,
Like soldiers, keeping watch upon the waves,
Protecting your own historic monuments
Placed strategically, as if on stage.

Glistening Granite City,
How proud you look to me.
Polished and honed to perfection.
Union Street, you haven't changed
For hundreds of years.
You've stood there through wars,
Celebrations and tears.

Glistening Granite City,
How I wish you could talk.
What would you tell me about those,
Who, through your streets have walked,
Past your glistening granite glory.
I can tell you have a story.

Glistening Granite City,
Were you born of Rubislaw Quarry,
disused and cast aside
Where once men worked with pride.

Glistening Granite City,
Aberdeen, you're made of this.
It is your badge of pride
You wear so well.
For each granite building
Has a story, someone tells.

Christine Nuttall

Trevelyan Cottage, Allithwaite

Pretty little cottage on a
Winding country lane
I look out my bedroom window
And see green fields again
But this is not my life
Only a short break
Just some relaxation as
A holiday I take.
Much needed, much enjoyed
Affording me much pleasure
Little house I will go home
But remember you forever.

Joan Todd

The Needles

Three gigantic molars
Jutting from the half-submerged jaw
Of prehistoric dinosaur,
Not predator, but friend;
Washed by Solent's gentle rollers
Atlantic tempest now no more,
While the far horizons lend
A sea-mist mantle of soft awe.
Farthest out a lighthouse stands
Safe and sure to welcome home
To their green and kindly own lands
Wanderers from far across the foam.

Barrie Williams

THE SURREY DAY

The sun rises slowly from the east
Her deep yellow manta fires the sky
As darkest black turns fiery blue
Golden embers deepen and lengthen
The cold shroud of night begins to fly

Mist Surrey shadows melt away
As the morning unwinds into day
By the waters begin to rise
Children begin to play

As the sun rises in the sky
The whitest of clouds float away
The fiery blue sky gleams alive
As a soft breeze gently blows
Brings life to the trees as they sway

At noon the morning burns away
As the afternoon is gently displayed
It leads the day into the breeze
As birds that sang the morning glory
Sing to the power of the afternoon shade

Long cool shadows colour the earth
And the children rest in the cool
While the clouds drift slowly by
The sun begins to say goodbye
As evenings siren calls to us all

The afternoon goes gently home
With tired happy faces in her wake
The suns fiery embers turn to red
As the evening call is finally said
Day says goodbye for night's sake

Her red and yellow fingers streak the sky
While the night begins her long call
And so the stars say a fond farewell
To the glory that is the end of this Surrey day
As she bids goodbye to us all

Colin Skilton

Cornwall's Changing Scene

Clenched fist of engine-house stands gaunt upon the hill,
Its chimney finger pointing heav'nward to the sky,
But crumbling now to show that time does not stand still,
And yet, a proud reminder of a time gone by.

Cornwall's sad echo of a great industrial past,
Though through the years, the elements have wreaked their worst,
Where useless scattered 'spoil' devoid of ore was cast
And Mother Nature's re-establishment seemed cursed.

But year by year, as humus fills between the stone,
And slowly, wind blown seeds create a gentler scene,
The germinating plants of gorse and heather grown
To paint the land with yellow, mauve and shades of green.

For those who owned the land, the mines created wealth
As world demand for Cornish tin and copper grew,
While others worked below with ever failing health;
To most of them, the only job they ever knew.

Though open mine shafts have so often now been capped,
Great caves and passages lie here beneath the soil
Of ancient workings, many never have been mapped;
A subterranean labyrinth from years of toil.

When dereliction ceases to offend the eyes;
The dun and brown of spoil shows hues of green instead,
Then future visitors may never realise
The honeycomb of holes and caves beneath their tread.

A Godman

SHAMROCK

The smell of peat burning on the hearth,
Reeked through the open cottage door
White walls, thatched roof
Set on an emerald green hill.

Before the door, the woman with a pail
Sat, and peeled potatoes for the stew
Her pinafore all muddy from the soil
Beyond, her husband in the distant bog
Cut peat in furrows, stacked to dry.

Small children ran about barefoot
Gathering flowers, some chased a ball.
Others sat beside the stream and fished
With stick and string, and net.

Soft turf did not hurt their feet
Only the marble glistening in the sun.
Connemara, they sang, Connemara
Home it is, and the heart sings on.

Joan Boswell

ALDWORTH GIANTS

Of Aldworth giants there are just nine,
And all in solid stone recline,
Here they pass their endless days,
In prayerful hope and silent praise.
Of Aldworth Castle not a trace,
The mound is there but not the place.
It seems ironic that they lie,
In castle keep of church nearby.
These Norman knights with William came,
To serve their king was all their aim,
But what with wars, crusades and routs,
The male line quickly fizzled out.
Now they're only left in stone,
They've made the church their final home.
In fact it could be said they're caught,
With feet in chancel, head in porch.
So much room they take within,
They cannot pack the village in.
They built another aisle to take,
Three more tombs for pity's sake.
Did they achieve the Heaven they sought,
Or was all this pomp and show for nought?

Graham K A Walker

WALES

Wales, Wales, this land of song
With Cardiff, it's Capital
It's civic centre to be admired
Its architecture inspired

Castles steeped in history
That once were graced with Royalty
Knights in armour and warriors bold
Many tales and legends unfold

Its coastline rocky, rugged and mountainous
Sloping to beaches of soft golden sand
Mountains and valleys adorn with a purpose
This terrain so rich, lush and verdant

Various foods of Welsh origin
Welsh cakes, lavar bread and leeks, to name a few
And the flower, so simple, yet so resplendent
Is the famous daffodil

Strange tales have been handed down
From generation to generation
Rites and rituals, weird premonitions
Folklore, ghosts and strange superstitions

The game of rugby takes pride of place
Deep in the heart of this Welsh race
Its people warm and friendly
Wales land of song, I embrace

Wales, Wales, land of song
Where the singing emanates from the soul
We sing with a passion right from the heart
Over which we have no control

Phyllis L Stark

DERWENT WATER AT DUSK

Clouds gather in the evening sky
Hanging like smoke in the pink glow of the dying sun,
And the hills seem to stand and wait
To hide countless secrets, now that the darkness of night has begun.

The Lake, gleaming rosily beneath the sky,
Fades into the shadows where it laps the brooding land,
And gentle ripples move the still waters
Where an outcrop of rock stretches in the lake like a giant hand.

All is quiet, only night creatures begin to stir;
The shadows change and deepen in the gleam of the fading light
And the breeze is no more than a passing sigh
As it skims the waters in the eerie silence of a lakeland night.

Win Wilcock

WOULDHAM

A quaint little village in Kent
Were many happy years with our family were spent,
All open land, and the river quite near
The trees all laden with fruit every year.

The cattle all grazed in the fields thick with grass
We waved to the folks on the bus when it passed,
The beautiful roses that grew round the door
The sweet smell of blossoms, who could ask for more.

The children would go to school every day
I would be busy while they were away,
Stories were told around the fire of a night
Then tucked up in bed, and a sweet kiss goodnight.

Flo E Smith

ENCHANTING PLACES

There are many enchanting places
To visit in Britain
That feels one with grace
That doth always remain

There are always attractions
For every one to enjoy
And there are no exceptions
For even one coy!

One enhances tranquillity
In the mountains
And in all reality
Often wish to remain

Now and then
One will find such pleasure
Boating on the 'River Thames'
Viewing passing scenery at leisure

There be plenty of sport
All year round
For thee to sought
Either on the sea or ground

One may find frivolity
Visiting public places
To fulfil their humidity
A 'flutter' at the horse races

So much to do and see
Oft' giving one a gasp
As folk will agree
And long may it last

Josephine Foreman

ON ORCHY BRIDGE

For let time pass
clearing anguish and doubt away
stay fast against the torrent.
A rock, stone or pebble within
remain yet allow,
the wearing away and ageing
for let time pass.

For it was willed that way
rivulets to meet and separate,
join again after memory fails
running away and eddying.
Relentless the flow of loving
for it was willed that way.

The bridge-crossed stream gathers
breath in the shadows,
gives a whispered insistence,
then flowing into light, exults
in the truth of its own existence.

Michael Alan Fenton

OUR MOTHERLAND

And must we sit and watch her glory fade,
   Who led the world to freedom years ago,
Watch city, town and village bow their heads,
   Subservient to laws which little know
   Or care, the heritage we still can show?

Fair land of England! We who shared the fight,
   And gave, from every household, of our best
To stem the growth of cruel tyranny,
   Who gave, against what odds, from east to west
   By glowing sun and gentle rain caressed.

Now choose, my heart, if such a choice can be,
   What place you hold the dearest of them all,
White cliffs of Dover; Ireland's verdant shores;
   Scotland's proud landscape; in Wales some waterfall,
   Or English meadows where the songbirds call?

Pause then on gardens, filled with summer flowers -
   The little ones which fringe the busy street;
The wide and gracious ones which soothe the soul,
   Offering rest to spirit and to feet,
   And patio and window box which neighbours greet.

Yours is the challenge now, youth of today;
   Be strong in friendship, worthy of our trust.
Hold freedom with compassion, tolerant faith,
   Serve our land foremost, lonely if you must,
   But make you sure that what you do is just.

Kathleen M Hatton

TRANQUILLITY

Sitting alone atop a field at Wythop Mill.
I watched the Herdwicks grazing below.
All was tranquil.

The stillness only broken by:
The wind rustling the leaves of the trees and bushes behind me.
The occasional bleat of a sheep and in the distance,
The swish of traffic as it sped along the A66.
Oblivious to the surrounding beauty.

From somewhere unseen, the echo of a woodpigeon.
The sheep move slowly about their field.
Pausing from their grazing momentarily,
To cast a cursory glance in my direction.
Thence returning to their unceasing chewing of grass.
I feel accepted and at one with the abundant nature all around me.

The sound of a plane high overhead, hidden by clouds,
Intrudes into my thoughts.
Suddenly, I realise it's grown cold and the evening shades are lengthening.
So, I wend my way home.
My footsteps slow and laboured, as I try to capture the moment
In my mind's eye forever.

B J Eyre

THE MOAT

You could smell the land an hour away,
as the ship throbbed homewards.
Burning stubble, above Compton bay,
made a pillar of smoke heavenwards
from the low hills of the island,
leading to our promised land.
Everywhere, white sails, like chips
off the cliffs beyond, and ships!
An orange roofed tug, a green tanker,
a blue fishing boat, a coaster at anchor.
Clouds closing on the land, fog banks out to sea,
green waves grading to a grey infinity.
Past forts and buoys threading our way,
the continent, the holiday, left behind,
home to adversity and glory declined.

Roger J Gould

WHERE WHITE WATERS FLOW

Near an old mine working,
in the valley just below.
Such a sight beholds you,
where white waters flow.

By side the track, and under trees,
a myriad of snowdrops sway,
in a gentle breeze.
Shy primrose down near waters edge,
re-affirms nature's age old pledge.

Spring is coming, summer, harvest too,
bringing new challenges, for me, for you.
Kernow is a wonderland, any time of year,
when forced at last to leave it, many shed a tear.

G J Von-Heizon

RAIN ON ARGYLE STREET

There is something about thunder and
 old shabby suburbs,
About cramped little houses and storm
 glittery streets,
About derelict sheds all the same as
 each other
And rusty old swing posts and wet garden
 seats.

There is something about gutters all
 leaky and gimcrack,
Of lights through the treetops all
 dismal and blurred,
Of small smoky rooms behind dusty net
 curtains,
Of old velvet sofas all lumpy and furred.

It's hard to explain quite the feeling
 it brought on me
Opening the window in dark drenching
 rain,
Watching the elm trees all drippy and
 dreary,
Hearing the water awash in the drain.

Hard to explain yet uncannily easy -
The strange mix of melancholy, hope
 and despair
Of gloominess mixed with ecstatic
 elation
On first hearing poetry whispering
 there.

Sarah Knox

FLATFORD

Crouching amid the bulrushes,
Standing with one hand on the gate.
Trying to get back into the past;
Born two centuries two late.

Scaffolding clings to the ancient wall.
Though they are lime-washing the cottage,
The closed door, the window small
And blank, look impervious to change.

Was old new then, is new old now?
In the sheltered valley of the Stour,
Where stately willows line the river,
There seems no sense of year or hour.

Change the hour, change the year:
The mill, the pond, the quiet lane
Remain. A young artist may appear,
And Willy Lott come home again.

Andria Jane Cooke

SIDMOUTH SOLILOQUY

Quiet seaside bays
I often frequented
In past summer days
Or autumn leaves
Impressed on me
A feeling of serenity.

Erstwhile fishing village
Eighteenth century
Houses broached
By progress march.

Now when holiday strikes
Your pleasant bays
And curses you with cars and bikes
While thronging crowds
Clutter up your ways
And loud transistor music
Shatters your fragile peace.

And sticklike travellers
Parade and fill the air
Fumed cider to their lips
Through straggled hair
And sing their folk songs
Softly to the sky.

The early early morning
Quietest time of all
To hear the wild seabirds
With their eerie mewling call
As I walk along the beach
Is the nearest ever
To paradise I'll reach.

Rupert Smith

NORTH WALES

When the silence brings its eerie hush,
And solitude prevails,
As the Red Kite soars to heavenly heights,
You know you're in North Wales.

Caernarfon and Conwy add historic charm,
And Beddgelert, of doubtless renown,
With Llandudno nestling peacefully,
Like a jewel, in Snowdonia's crown.

The golden light of summer shines,
In a daily, majestic display,
Anointing the children's blissful sands,
From Prestatyn, to Red Wharf Bay.

This wind, this breeze, so cool and kind,
These countless streams and rapid falls,
This generous land, so ready to deliver,
As the sea, tides its way, up the Conwy river.

Like a diamond in a hail of light,
Enriching sea and sand and sails,
From Llangollen you begin to see,
The splendour, of North Wales.

Dennis Scott

THE HOMEWARD CALL

This ancient land both gentle and strong,
has a vitality to outlive the years long.
Advance and progress may make its mark,
yet Ireland authentic shall stand out stark.
Its resounding walls tell of its rich history,
while the silent mists cling tight with mystery.
Its skilfully woven patchwork quilt of green
folds gently in to inspire our dreams.
Why could anyone seek to have more
when contentment exists just beyond our door.
Yet many have rebelled and sought to roam,
only to find themselves in a foreign land alone.
On the banks of that shore they patiently listen,
and to Ireland's echoing call they freely hasten.
For like the children of Lir,
they shall not stray far from waters held dear.

Sharon Ferguson

TALLY HO!

The days when Britain was G-B will shortly be no more.
No longer ruling waves and tides as they erode our shore.
The politicians, *oh so wise* are eroding from within.
Our pound, upon which we have built, will soon be in the bin.
Our thousand year traditions like hunting with the hounds,
will be declared illegal and by twits made out of bounds.
The idiots who built 'The Dome' are boobing yet again
by cutting down the pleasures of all the countrymen.
Because a tiny group of prats have loudly uttered voice
and with bombs and thefts of animals are forcing through *their* choice.
Our politicians, *oh so wise,* are heeding to the few
forgetting that the many may not vote for them anew.
Remember, though, that stupid laws are never set and sealed.
Just like the Corn Laws in the past, they can always be repealed.

D G W Garde

THE 1ST OF MARCH

Around Wales they can be seen
When we dress in our Welsh way
Golden daffodils and leeks of green
We wear them on Saint David's Day.

Little boys in flat caps
Bright red waistcoats looking smart
Little girls in tall top hats
Shawls and aprons with skirts of plaid.

Choirs sing with great Welsh voices
Anthems and ballads to make you cry
The whole of Wales rejoices
For our Saint will never die.

Red dragon flags are flying high
The greatest symbol of Welsh pride
Unique Welsh warmth you just can't buy
It makes you feel so good inside.

Around Wales in every corner
You will see us celebrate
On the 1st of March we will honour
Dearest David our patron Saint.

Marie Horridge

SPREADING CHESTNUT TREE (EVELITH-SHROPSHIRE)

'Neath Evelith's spreading chestnut tree
Standing here, we will be free
Boughs outreaching far and wide
See the horses' side by side

Glistening brook flows gently by
With banky meadow stretching high
Grasses grow 'twixt meadow flowers
Trees are tall, such regal towers

King Charles' oak grows to the right
In woodland where he hid that night
The long redundant paper mill
Country home does stand there still

Woodland path for you to walk
Nettles on their lengthy stalks
Leads you on to Kemberton Mill
With history, if you have the will

Look across the meadow green
Canada geese, they're to be seen
Spending summer in this place
Until the winter they must face

If you're lucky, along the stream
Your eyes will catch the bluest gleam
A kingfisher makes his speedy flight
Keeping a fish within his sight

Mentioned in the Doomsday Book
Why not take time and have a look?
And see awesome beauty, as I do
I know your heart will breathe anew!

Ester Francisca Caruana

Co Down

If you ever go to Ireland, you must pay a visit to Co Down
The people are always happy there, you'll never see a frown
Swim in the sea at Newcastle, but be careful you don't drown
Then after that you can always take a wee trip round the town.

The majestic Mourne Mountains are a must for you to see
They've been featured many times on Ulster's daytime TV
They sharply rise up to the sky then gently slope down to the sea
Spending the day just looking at them seems like heaven to me.

If it's golden sands you're looking for then visit Tyrella Beach
So relax and enjoy the quiet because heaven's just within your reach
It doesn't matter who you go with there'll be something there for each
And it all looks so tranquil that you are sometimes robbed of speech.

The City of Belfast is close by its less than 40 miles away
So hop on an Ulster bus and go and visit it for the day
Be sure to see St Anne's Cathedral if you feel the need to pray
The Ulster Museum and City Hall visit them too without delay.

The shopping arcades sell everything you could ever possibly need
There's no security checks now, so you can do it all at great speed
Pick one of the colourful cafes if you're hungry and want a big feed
Don't worry about the troubles, don't believe everything that you read.

The Harland and Wolf shipyard was once a very important place
Even though the Titanic sunk, the shipyard can still show its face
They're still proud to have built it, they don't feel any disgrace
The good thing about Belfast is it refused to join the rat race.

Maggie Fairbrace

HOLIDAY IN CORNWALL

Here in Cornwall, troubles are few
Come and travel a mile or two,
A seaside town that's known as Looe
Sell fish and chips, a dream come true,
Sailing and fishing boats moored nearby
Are a beautiful sight under a summer sky,
On the quay side, fish for crab
It's fun for children, mum and dad,
To Tintagel you must head
Land of legends and King Arthur fame,
You will be really glad you came.

To Rock and Polzeath, with time on your hands
Near Daymer Bay once buried by sands,
St Enodoc church still proudly stands
In its graveyard one of the best
Sir John Betjamen was laid to rest,
He wrote poems as times were lean
His title, 'Poet Laurete' to our Queen.

Worth a visit St Michael's Mount
Approached by beach when the tide is out,
Visit Newquay, the park and zoo
Are memories to take home with you,
There's such a lot to see and do
Here in Cornwall waiting to view
Can we look forward to seeing you?

Sheila Walters

MY SENTIMENTAL JOURNEY

A mellow breeze cools the midday sun,
contentment soothes my soul
as I glimpse beloved Bredon Hill.
Footsteps of old I trace again,
each stone a tale to tell
of this idyllic place.

Over the stile, into the leafy shade
of the ancient quarry.
Sounds of silence echo around me,
memories flicker before my eyes.
The majestic Malverns, verdant pastures,
Elgar's land of hope and glory.

Wearily the dusty path I trek,
neat furrowed fields, vivid wild flowers.
Quietly pausing, God's creation to bless.
Drifting midst lofty skies, the sun
sheds golden rays over the folly.
Elated, on the summit I stand.

Close to nature, a feeling of peace,
far below, a breathtaking view of
the river Avon, winding its silver trail
through plains and patchwork fields.
Deep in thought, a voice is calling,
'Come back, come back to Bredon Hill.'

Diana Frewin

BLAKEDEAN MOOR

Postage stamp fields of
green, yellow and brown,
Pastoral landscape of
hills and down,
Valleys beneath the moss
covered hillside and rocks,
cradle the stream, flowing
life's blood underneath
bridges of bygone ages,
have stood the passage of time.

A tree stretches out its
branches, like arthritic fingers
and catches my hair
in a tangled mess.
A dog barks in the distance,
a sheep looks up startled
ready to run.
'Stay my dear, let me weave
your coat of fine wool to keep
me warm in winter.'

On these wind swept moors
the bracken dies for a
thousand reasons, protects
and shields new seedlings
from Jack Frost's fingers.

Kath Gabbitas

THE HAMPSHIRE DOWN

Of all the places of great renown
One must have heard of the Hampshire Down.
Southwards it slopes down to the sea
And northwards descends to lush country,
With sleepy hamlets - oft seen in dreams,
Midst leafy woods and bubbling streams
And verdant fields and winding lanes,
All freshened by the season's rains.
But if one likes the sea and ships
And summer fun and seaside dips,
Then one must visit our great resorts
And watch or play our national sports.
Enjoy our history unsurpassed
When visiting places of the past,
Such as castles and parks - all of fame;
Which help to build up Hampshire's name.
Why should its citizens deign to roam
When all their pleasures are at home?
Pray Heavenly Father when I die
May I be buried 'neath Hampshire's sky.

Douglas Wood

EDINBURGH - GOD'S CITY

I saw God's angel stoop to kiss
This city of terrestrial bliss,
As there among its verdant hills,
The borough of Eden gently spills.
Surely a city like none other
With gentle heart beats of a mother.

And then the cherub placed his feet
Most solemnly on 'Arthur's Seat'
As with a trumpet salutation,
He sounded forth this declaration,
'This city shall forever be
A place of love and liberty.'

So visiting the 'Royal Mile'
Where gracious buildings seem to smile,
And every stone leaps out to tell
The history it knows so well.
Their pageantry of every kind
Invades the portals of the mind.

So in this time-warp we bestride,
Let's tell the truth and nothing hide.
For, from this city, still today
The blood washed saints, show forth the way,
With many prayers and intercession,
Tell folk the truth of sin's transgression.

Then every day let's surely greet
This city standing on its feet,
To sing the praises of our God,
Who moulded man from humble sod.
'Auld Reekie' built on hills full seven,
It could be that we're twinned with Heaven!

I H Davies

THE WAY татO EMMANUEL

Should you chance to visit Swindon,
Brunel's railway town of Wiltshire
. . . or it was until the eighties,
And it still is to the faithful,
At the northern end you'll find us
Waiting in a fertile valley,
Waiting there to bid you welcome
To a place called Haydon Wick.

Old indeed, parts of the village,
Old indeed, the records show,
Quiet and peaceful notwithstanding
Changes that have made it grow,
Pushing local boundaries eastwards
To encompass Greenmeadow
(I should know for we have lived here,
Oh, for thirty years or so).

At the centre of the village,
At its centre, at its heart,
Stands the church (some call it chapel)
With an orchard rimmed by flowers.
What a metaphor for Eden!
What a symbol of God's care!
That a church and apple orchard
Jointly stand to serve Him there.

Step inside and you'll discover
Words engravened, 'God With Us',
Showing how the people worship
Trusting in the Saviour's love,
Steadfast in their Christian witness,
Welcoming to all who come,
Giving praise to God the Father
And to Jesus Christ, His Son,
Drawing on the Holy Spirit,
One in Three and Three in One.

Sheila Burnett

A Flickered Light

Is there still a glow, or has it gone out?
Is there a hope or chance, or is it at
a glance or to look in?
To look through a window or to walk
through a door before it closes, but it
could be more.
A flickered light you see in sight, the
window could break and the door to close.
A moment in time a hesitation of thought,
for the future could be in sight.
But don't be blind for there is still room to
see, a flickered light will come to thee.

S Hamilton

THOUGHTS OF LONG AGO

One day I went to the Wallace Collection,
They really have a most rare selection
Of beautiful paintings and furniture fine,
Tapestry old, but of quaint design.
Armour of splendour and shining brass,
China of beauty and sparkling glass.
Masses of clocks were dotted around,
And here and there a mirror was found.
Though common enough these things may be,
They certainly painted a picture for me.

As I mounted the stairs, my mind brought to life
A picture of beauty, yet, trouble and strife.
I saw fine ladies in silk and in lace,
Yet each had a look of distress on their face.
Men of high living were standing around,
But each in their turn seemed to murmur and frown.
As I moved through the rooms, I knew they were there,
I could feel them staring from every chair.
I saw them using the china and glass,
The furniture, armour and shining brass.
They seemed to live in a world of their own.
This beautiful house, was the place they called home.
And all therein did their wishes comply,
Their clothes were the finest that money could buy.
And yet, 'midst this picture of grandeur and state,
The atmosphere hung with mistrust, fear and hate.
Though they had all the riches and pleasures of earth,
Their lives were empty of love, peace or mirth.
While their hearts were groping for higher things,
Their minds knew only the pleasures life brings.

Sandra J Walker

SECRECY OF BYGONE DAYS

Grey stone walls in sombre silence stand
Holding secrets of bygone days
Witnessed the bravery of slaving hands
Who piled the hewn stones on high.

Ivy curling around the stately tower
Concealing bell that peels no more to
Welcome morning worshippers
Belfry invaded with sleeping bats
Their lofty environment undisturbed.

Graveyard marked with ancient tombs
Flowers displayed here and there
Revealing evidence ancestors visit the
Sacred ground, beneath a yew tree
I read aloud, five children of same family
Died within one week
The famine year of 1845 reaping
A harvest of weary starving souls.

Standing in reverence I catch a glimpse,
Of long ago, how hard to watch those
Little children die, I shed a tear,
Could we reap a cruel harvest like this
again, scraping the moss from granite tomb
I read the words 'To God be the Glory'
Yet this man buried entire family.
Leaving words of faith eternally.

F Gibson

YORKSHIRE WONDERLAND

Alice arrived from the U S of A
With her relatives she came to stay.
In rainy Bradford - that's not by the sea.
Where there's muck, there's brass - feel free,
To sample the fare in large amounts,
A piece of England is all that counts.
Three weeks vacation, seems plenty of time,
So even if the sun doesn't shine,
The places of interest are varied and rare,
Leeds, Haworth, Keighley, where most people care.
York with its museums, Sheffield's great Meadowhall,
Blackpool with its Tower, that's ever so tall.
Illuminating everything against the night sky,
Like a child in wonderment, we hear Alice cry!
It's beautiful, it's marvellous, please take my hand,
Lead me on, show me more of this!
Strange Wonderland . . .

Bernice Sharpe

GREEN VALLEY GRASS

My valley once was clothed in green
Enjoyed by all; idyllic scene.
But all too soon black gold was found
Beneath the grass, well underground.

Then people came from far and wide
To work in that fine countryside.
They tore the grass from its fine roots.
In vain grass tried to form new roots.

The mountain tops soon turned jet black.
The green was gone, no turning back.
For families found work just there.
Exploited, life was never fair.

Beneath the grass one fateful sound
Meant many died there underground.
How long would that injustice last?
The dice for them had there been cast.

So many hoped each day for change,
For green upon the mountain range.
Change came at last, but what a price.
A pill quite bitter never nice.

The pits have disappeared from sight.
Few jobs around, a fearful plight.
Then factories brought work and change.
Slag heaps torn from the mountain range.

This area calls me each year
To return home full of good cheer.
Still poverty is all around.
But friendliness is always found.

My valley once again is green.
I marvel at the wondrous scene.

Catherine Craft

HOLIDAY IN WHITLEY BAY

I had a wonderful holiday,
In the town of Whitley Bay,
Each day the sun shone from a sky of blue,
Reflecting on the sea a similar hue.

I saw St Mary's Island with lighthouse grand,
And walked upon the golden sand,
I trotted to the end of Tynemouth Pier,
In the county of Tyne & Wear.

I saw Collingwood's monument so tall,
And the sunken garden at Wallington Hall,
There was one thing I didn't do though,
And that was to ride on the old Metro.

Once again my heart is longing to be,
In that place where the sky meets the sea,
On earth there is no town so fair,
Because the one I love lives there!

Pauline Wilkins

THIS TIMELESS LAND

Colourful counties,
   Wonderful views,
History, mystery,
   Heaven to choose.

Would Shakespeare have walked
   In the Forest of Arden,
Its beauty inspiring
   A magical garden?

The creator of Alice
   Perhaps still admires
His much loved city
   Of dreaming spires.

To the Garden of England
   Good pilgrims came,
Long before towns
   Of Dickensian fame.

Great writers and poets
   Have all had their say,
In this timeless land,
   Which is ours today.

J M Armstead

My Potted Plant

Of many colours
This land is made,
Gently blending as one.

The wretcherous sea,
The cloud filled sky,
The glowing morning sun.

Yet the beauty seen,
Of fields so green,
Brings forth my longing home.

So myself I surround,
With potted plants,
Bringing back comforts deep sown.

I fool myself,
But my heart somehow knows,
In my eyes, where it shows,
That the magic is more,
Than my potted plants,
This place captured by my heart.

Dawna Mechelle

CANTERBURY

Steeped in English history,
Canterbury stands strong against time.
Dominated by the Cathedral,
Where pilgrims still come to pray.
The city walls now lay in ruins,
A reminder of a different age.
Here once stood a Roman town,
Today it is buried beneath the ground.
A Roman museum holds the relics,
And displays a long lost way of life.
Canterbury takes pride in its heritage,
And salutes the town's Roman roots.
The market still attracts the masses,
Aided by the many and varied shops.
Locals mingle freely with tourist,
Sometimes hard to identify by sight.
A thriving town, a tourist dream,
One of the many that make England great.
Where else in this vast world,
Can people boast such a history?

M A Challis

IF THEY RETURNED (FROM THE PAST)

If they returned what would they see?
A river once dirty now flowing free.
Multiplying rushes caressing the bank,
Where rainbowed oil films once prevalent and rank.

If they returned they would not view
The pit wheel controlling the unseen crew,
But set to sight in a concrete base,
A reminder of many a grimy face.

If they returned they would find rare,
The wild flower and the songbird fair,
But rubbish strewn the leafy lane,
Where thoughtlessness creates the strain.

If they returned they would find whole,
The efforts of replacing coal.
Factory units standing fine,
Heralding new working time.

If they returned much change they'd see.
A way of life that's come to be.
Changes made, the past now fading
And custom of a newer trading.

Life departs life, we stand in time,
Conscious of our present clime.
If we returned we may find a race,
Living long in outer space.

Let's live for now and yet progress.
To make our lives a great success.
Building a community we should afford,
If they returned would they applaud?

Walter Crooks

MEMORIES OF ENGLAND

I remember a time in England so green
Hardly a motor car was ever seen.
When butterflies decorated Earth so bright
And open doors were left alright.
When children roamed woods at ease
And fish were always found in England's seas.
When love was given instead of lust
And helping thy neighbour was always a must.
When Beachy Head was a sight to see
And not an end to those who don't want to be.
I remember Christmases with little, but rich.
The joy of my old bike when I was a tich.
The smell of fresh cakes baked by my mum
And the happiness because I had made some.
Pineapple chunks, sweats I can still taste,
Pig men picking up our leftovers waste.
Rag and Bone men singing for wares,
Chatting to a policeman who really cares.
Open fires and that smell of coal
And that Old England's Fathers role.
The slowness of old England's pace
Not like today's break neck race.
How I miss that old England so,
Where on Earth did it go?

Pete Simmons

THE SILVER BIRCH

Slender is the silver birch
Boughing branches hang with dignity
Beside the small country church
Shimmering leaves glowing with serenity.

As dancing shadows lurk
Over the windows' stained coloured glass
And ancient biblical quirk
On a plaque of shiny brass.

Trunk of polished grey bark
As the tall spire
Rises with the lark
Astonishing sunrise tangerine fire

The church clock strikes three
The songbird consecrated high on the holy tree.

Ann Copland

THE GREATNESS OF BRITAIN

This segment of Europe broken free
With such a wealth of diversity.
Great character by its people drawn
To so many new horizons borne.

Wherever fate has made them stand
Britain is their green and pleasant land.
No where else on earth quite so fair
Than this homeland that they all share.

It is so very small in actual size
Within its shores lies a great surprise.
From white cliffs, across the Weald
Runnymede's Magna Carta sealed.

So many freedoms were secured here
That have been nurtured for many a year.
On this isle there is much to gain
With the institutions that remain.

From John O'Groats to Land's End
Many united peoples can blend.
Being British is that compromise
Which allows all that's best to rise.

A land without desert or jungle
No volcanoes or earthquakes rumble
But there's a great contrast in style
On this our unpretentious isle.

So many aspects that are unique
A language for a world to speak.
It's separate development allowed
Such a distinction from the crowd.

Our 'Demi Paradise' is right here
Our 'Sceptred Isle' that is so dear.

H D Hensman

SEEING RABBITS FROM THE TRAIN

Silver rabbits in the dawn
like soap bubbles,
sitting so still,
leaving the gossamer undisturbed.

Thundering under the mist,
a pine-fresh train
zipping green velvet,
Penzance to Paddington.

A day of hammers,
heads and hot heels,
and roads to rabbitless parks.

Evening. A softer train,
smelling of chocolate,
rollicking home
through richer velvet,
finding the silver rabbits turned to gold.

Sheila Jeffries

FOR LIFE

Can a man love for life - the same beauty,
As an English view?
A silent moment
When the sun waves goodbye;
On rolling hills and nature's eye.

Can a man love for life - the ageless concern
Of an English prom?
The burning warmth
Of a fiddler's bow;
That stirs the spirit both high and low.

Can a man love for life - the sweet copulation
Of an English ale?
The scented smell
Of burning leaves;
That dance with memory and summer breeze.

Can a man love for life - the sacred bed,
Of England's past?
It's prosperous forests
In which to roam;
An ethereal palace that stands alone.

Oh my merry England!
Do not cast me aside at death
Let me roam your hills instead - a crowning moment of nature's balm;
That quells the fire and brings the calm.
On my merry England!

S P Springthorpe

MAYFIELD, SUSSEX

This place I love with all my heart.
Though I may move, yet here I dwell . . .
For of my being, Mayfield's one part.

If I would try my life to chart
Elsewhere . . . The call comes like a bell.
This place I love with all my heart.

The longing pierces like a dart;
Such sad nostalgia I can't quell -
For of my being, Mayfield's one part.

The wrench of leaving makes me smart:
Nowhere but here could I be well.
This place I love with all my heart.

If I must go, and live apart,
I'll hold this memory in a shell,
For of my being, Mayfield's one part.

To sing its praise I lack the art,
So gladly I'd its glories tell.
This place I love with all my heart,
For of my being, Mayfield's one part.

Katharine Holmström

NORTHUMBERLAND LANDSCAPE

Quiet wide water-colour skies
clouds lowering to rising hills
the changing quality of light.

Fitful the seeking wind
sounding through leaves, wafting
the scent of hedgerow honeysuckle

Easing
the blessing of certain constancies:
steadfastness of trees,
the visible permanence of stone,

sudden radiance.

Louise Rogers

SUSSEX, MY SUSSEX

Come back, you fields of pale-green waving corn,
Strewn with your poppies, blood-red in the morn,
With mayweed, charlock, cornflowers sapphire-blue,
And nodding marigolds of brighter hue.

Come back, you skylark, trilling out your praise,
Rising to heav'n in April's azure haze.
And come back, gentle plover, to your rest,
Crouched in the furrowed earth on fragile nest.

And come, you hedgerows, white with hawthorn flower,
All graced with blossom for a maiden's bower.
And come back too when autumn's south wind blows,
With scarlet haws and hips, and purple sloes.

And all you meadows, resting now in May,
With myriad wild flowers, thriving mid the hay:
With buttercup and vetch and meadowsweet
And tiny cinquefoil 'neath the fox's feet.

Yes, come back, all you fields and meadows gay.
Untouched by pesticide and poison spray.
And come back honey bee and damsel fly,
Whose labour answers ev'ry farmer's cry.

Yes, come back, ev'ry joy of former days
And ev'ry memory of the gentle ways.
Transform our Sussex Downs, our clay bound Weald,
Our Forest Ridge with patchwork shaw and field,
Our river valleys where the car is king,
Our fields of sterile wheat - where no birds sing.

Transform our countryside - yes, make it clean,
And bless our land with a more gracious scene.

Ken Brown

ST EDMUND

In an ancient monastery in an olde market town in the shire of Suffolk
An oath by the barons of the land was sworn and peace was born.
Of chain mail and roses an Oath to the magna carta.
In Bury St Edmunds town the plight of St Edmund
King of the east angles he defied the Danes by refusing to be their
Puppet on the throne as the Danish king wanted Edmunds throne.
All that Edmund surveyed the Danish king craved.
This show of defiance split St Edmunds alliance
      though in the beckoning
light St Edmund was close to God he was a renowned sight.
By the flowing river Lark he contemplated his plight.
His army was defeated but hand on his heart his faith
      in God it did not depart
after an ultimatum by the Danish king he despatched an army
to cut the head off Edmund the East angles king.
The Danish troops trussed him up and shot him with arrows
after Edmund refusing to defy his faith he became
      St Edmund the martyred king.
In Bury St Edmunds many a tale has been told about him.

Jonathan Covington

LAND OF HOPE AND GLORY?

Land of hope and glory?
Let me tell you now, a different story
We live not in a land of hope and glory
But more a land of dope and the more gory, instead
Dream on dreamer, and you the ardent
Schemer, for this land is more full, of
Insecurity and dread
Fine it would be, to ring out, believe you me
And of some said glory
Fine it would be, to tell you all, a very different story
But let's face the facts, we live in a world
Not only hoary, but oh so inglorious instead
Where, dope, not hope is surely bred
And the only glory of it, is dead, to you
I can sing, and such sweet notes to this world bring
Land of hope and glory! Ping, ping, goes another life
God forgotten, Christ forgotten, all so conservative is
It? Ring, ring, who has been stung again, oh strife!

Margaret Lightbody

BREAD FROM EVANS

I lived in Tonyrefail once,
Up in Glamorgan shire,
And bombs or not, they sang and sang -
Treorchi's Male Voice Choir!

I lived behind a butcher's shop,
As prices mounted higher,
My uncle made a fortune from
Treorchi's Male Voice Choir.

My cousin came to stay awhile,
(The Cardiff Blitz was dire!)
She slept out in the shelter with
Treorchi's Male Voice Choir.

I thought my Dad was being brave,
In trench and mud and mire,
But rumour had it, he was in
Treorchi's Male Voice Choir.

I lived in Tonyrefail once,
Up in Glamorgan shire,
And I can tell you something strange
About that famous choir,

Because our lads were waging war,
Treorchi's Male Voice Choir,
Was ten Italians, seven Poles,
Five Yanks - and Mrs Dyer!

Peter Davies

SLAVANKA

Once of Russian Aristocracy, now of Godly, royalty,
Because this is a place, where the King is met.
In wonderful soothing surroundings,
Beautiful rooms, fill Slavanka.
Furnished using such good taste, so comfortable,
Moreso, Jesus' beauty is captivated in this place.

As one moves through the building,
You realise that it is built, on the solid rock of Salvation
There is tranquillity, a spiritual peace,
A feeling of communion, and a gentleness.
Joy is present, it's not the bricks and mortar
That hold and bind us, or the architecture,
But, the heart, which beats at Slavanka.

Evenly silently, drawing the residents together,
Into refreshing fellowship with one another
A short time of refuge, and rest,
Then it's time to move on, and walk the path
That God has set before you
Until the next time!

Louise White

SILENT SPRING
(In memory of all the sentient beings slaughtered due to the foot and mouth outbreak 2001 - special thoughts for the unemployed sheep dogs)

Dark red grass
heralds a silent spring
for the birds do not sing
in respect of the dead
that lay blackened
for the killing fields
of Great Britain
are testimony to
man's slaughter
of the innocent.

Anita Richards

DERRY'S ICY TIDE

This morning woke with piercing fog -
the winter grass a field of spears, glinting
in the subdued sunlight,
hinting of the glorious vista I here log;
whispering the wonder.

Keen, excited eyes found no fault
in panorama now fast revealing
sea of eddying white,
appealing in its beautiful tender assault,
leaving town asunder . . .

broken in the sense that downtown
slid beneath the shrouding waves which crashed on
the city's graded height,
choked on the swallow that the suburbs would have downed.
Awed, I watched this wonder -
and praised the author!

Perry McDaid

AUTUMN AT DAY'S LOCK

The year end colours are so beautiful.
I long to take a pair of secateurs on walks
to gather up the gold and rusty leaves
and scarlet fruits, but I'm unsure
how much of this is Nature's Bounty
and how much the farmer's.

The hedges on the footpath to the lock
are full of pinky-orange spindle berries.
I'd love to place a jug full of them
glowing in my hearth
to warm the cooling evenings.
Brambles are ripe with blackberries
and the heavy bells of elderberries
weigh their branches down.
Copious purple droppings show
that birds and animals (less concerned
than I about whose property this is)
have feasted freely on the generous glut.

My autumn coloured dogs
are also harvesting the hedgerows
and, to date, have brought me
two crow-pecked rabbits,
one half dead pigeon
and - most treasured trophy -
one long dead Canada goose.

Carolyn Garwes

AN ENGLISH DELIGHT

To wander far on moonlit night
Across moors, dank and silent
With floating mist surrounding, a fright
Hills that slowly wander down to coves, with intent
To capture the atmosphere of smugglers bent
On giving kinsmen a run,
From Cornwall inlets to Dorset caves,
Gives me a smell of musket and gold.
Hearts beating fast, to land caskets, amid waves,
Pounding old England shores, thro' rocks and sound,
Their interest to achieve, one aim profound
Along slippery seaweed shores, this band.
Conflict growing as armed tunics, strike the sand.
Fighting to give man's share to govern the land
Local men from accents broad in size
Things, our rugged outline boast
A resentment of constraint, giving rise
A pride, these men, along our coast
Led England to freedom. So wise
Men give reasons, but actions we toast
These moors and bogs hold memories, we boast
England survives with heritage
      While other nations aswage.

Albert Boddison

OLD INGESTRE

Each English county claims some startling place,
and old Ingestre, near Stafford, stakes its own.
Surprise is momentary and fact endures.

Tie up a narrow boat near Tixall's fields
visit the famous Gate House then proceed
To Doomsday Book's 'Gestreon' to find the church.

St Mary gives this Parish Church her name;
the Trent meanders and beyond the nearby parkland
on local grassy meadows cows stand grazing.

The Royal Society's rooms heard Chetwyn's plan,
the grandson of the Knight who built the Hall
for it was he and Dr Plot who summoned Wren.

Great minds conferred within their learned sphere;
but only this one church beyond London's bounds
is known to be Sir Christopher's own design.

The architect, Archbishop and young Chetwyn
concurred, devised, began another scheme
in 1673 to build this quiet, gracious, holy place.

Throughout four years all craftsmen plied their trades
before the local Bishop blessed and praised their toil
and was entertained quite splendidly at table.

Royal names from history centre on this plot,
Wren's masons' names, linked with St Paul's, are here
and Gibbons' hands most likely carved the wood.

Glass makers of renown, too, show their talents;
a one-handed clock turns on the squat bell tower,
but the loyal love of parishioners maintains.

Dennis Marshall

Rainbow

R adiant smiles on faces shine
A s arcs of colour paint the skies
I n the mix of rain and fine.
N one who pause to raise their eyes
B ehold the bow, earth crowned by line
O bserve with wonder, thinking, wise,
W alk on untouched by Heaven's sign.

Eve Devenish-Meares

THE KINGDOM OF LIGHT
(THE ARDNAMURCHAN PENINSULA)

We came at dusk to Ardnamurchan
As the long silver evening dimmed towards night.
Still sun's last glimmer fingered the gun-metal water,
For this is the kingdom of light.

We woke rinsed clean to the morning.
Under cloud's rim squint and glint of bright
Dazzled and danced on the glass of the loch's surface,
Claiming the kingdom of light.

We turned at noon to the great headland,
A tantrum of rain drumming the road out of sight.
But the doomsday sky was graced by a double rainbow:
A revelation of light.

We are caught and held by the last lighthouse.
Slow turning years dowse fantasies in flight.
Come to the wind's edge, we will show you glory
Unending: the gift of the kingdom of light.

Shaan Everson

SINNERS

Broughton entertained many missionaries in the 40s.
Why they came from America to Broughton, I don't know.
We didn't have a surfeit of sinners. I couldn't think of one.
With a population of 1000; there wouldn't be a big haul.
Neither did we have poor people. I couldn't think of one.

The missionary came to our church school
And gave us a red cardboard posting box.
They suggested that we post the names
Of all the poor people in the village
And on Sunday in church we would pray for them.

After the preacher went away; it was our Headmaster
Who suggested that there were no poor in Broughton.
He was right. There were people with less money;
But no actual poor. The preacher would be disappointed.

I don't know who put the Headmaster's name in the poor box
But we all knelt and prayed that God would feed him.
And on the Monday morning I stood in line
With all the other gigglers from the back pew,
Whose titters echoed around the church on Sunday.

We all received two smacks of the cane, on each hand.
We found out that there were some sinners in Broughton
And those missionaries, had come all the way from America
To catch us.

Ray Ford

SCHILLER AT MINACK

In this amphitheatre
High above the sea,
Open to the night sky,
We wait expectantly.

Pagan the beauty here -
Echoes of ancient Greece:
Crag and headland,
Wildness, peace.

The clouds are pink,
The sun red,
Sinking to rest
In watery bed.

Sea birds nestle
On the waves' crest.
The moonlight, golden,
Comes to rest,

Making a smooth path
On the ocean. Still
We sit here, you and I,
And drink our fill

Of poetry from
The lamplit stage.
Passion, ecstasy,
Love, rage,

As Mary Stuart,
Ill-fated queen,
Lives again in
A Celtic scene:

A summer night to have, to hold
Through the years as we grow old.

Jacqueline Abendstern

FLORA ORCADENSIS

Homeland, place on Earth where born,
trials, tribulations ever there - mourn,
here I will lay beneath a red and windswept sky,
so if I am lucky as those before do
there is no place reserved for you.

The valley of green, the sea, the rocks
a place to be, I thank my luck socks,
with coloured glory past, in saga told
the book of pages yet unfold.

With cotton summer stood in sun, like silk
in part there - of my birthright of that ilk.
No land of honey sure, fish and cows and milk.

J M Heddle

UK SOVEREIGNS: A BRIEF HISTORY

It all began with three Saxon Kings from 955 to 1016, with pride,
Edwy, Edgar, Edward-a Martyr, Unready Ethelred and
                                    Edmund Ironside,
then from 1017 to 1040 by three Danish Kings, two with funny names,
they were Canute, Harold I and Hardicanute and none were the same,
1042 to 1066, two Saxon Kings, Edward the Confessor and Harold II,
1066 to 1135 with two Williams, Henry I and Stephen fate beckoned,
The House of Plantagenet from 1154 to 1377, with eight kings anew,
Henry and Richards I and II, with John and three Edwards, all true,
from 1399 to 1422 came the House of Lancaster, after
                                      twenty-two years,
with a single name thrice repeated in this realm, all regal peers,
three kings named Henry, IV, V and VI, followed each other for sure,
the House of York from 1461 to 1483, three kings, names before,
they were in order again, Edward IV and V, and then Richard III,
and came the House of Tudor, from 1485 to 1558, these you
                                      have heard,
Henry VII and VIII, Edward VI, Mary and Elizabeth I, the first queens,
the daughter of Anne Boleyn, and the eighth king Henry, it seems,
followed by the House of Stuart, from the years 1603 to 1625,
with James I (James the VI of Scotland), and Charles I, kings revived,
then the 'Commonwealth', declared in 1649, and lasted from
                                      1653 to 1658,
two kings, Oliver Cromwell - Lord Protector and Richard Cromwell
                                      await,
and a restored House of Stuart, which lasted between 1660 and 1702,
Charles and James II, William III and Mary II together and Anne too,
and then came the House of Hanover from 1714 to 1837, so glorious,
with Georges I to IV, and William IV reign, followed by
                                      Queen Victoria's,
the brief House of Saxe-Coburg-Gotha, which only occurred in 1901,
this time a king named Edward VII, and this sovereign was the
                                      only one,

and then the Royal House of Windsor, which was 1910 to the present day, George V, Edward VIII, George VI and now Elizabeth II, in order this way.

Christopher Higgins

VALE OF AVALON

A silver mist hangs like a shroud over the quiet vale
It's called to man since time began, each inch could tell a tale
This place, this gem, this Avalon, King Arthur's resting place
There at his feet lay Guinevere, she once so fair of face
Sixteen feet down inside the earth in hewn-out tree of oak
Near where the wattle church once stood, that Joseph once bespoke
The holiest earth in England, our first English church
Where Joseph came to set his staff, a sign for you and me
St Michael's church upon the Tor surveys with silent gaze
Majestic Tor, mysterious hill, shrouded in a haze
It's called to man since time began, a strange uncanny pull
There's something still upon that hill, of magic, it is full
From ancient time to modern, when hippies come to view
They wait for things to happen, so should we wait too?

Dora Watkins

UK's Countryside Panorama

UKs countryside stands alone,
Ever differing shades of green,
A perpetually verdant zone
From plateau to mountainous scene.

Hills, dense forests, heaths and meadows,
Daubed coloured clumps, wild flower blooms,
Bluebell oceans ripple to and fro,
Springtime relief from leafage gloom.

Glinting rivers meander sketch,
Random duck ponds speckle vista,
Streams cast a scintillating fine stretch
Lakes, locks, iridescent glister.

Hamlets where ancient inns abound,
Village cricket team wearing 'whites',
Leather clicks willow, distinctive sound,
Both customary rural sights.

Centuries-old churches dot view,
Flagstones well-worn by countless feet,
Doors hand-grooved turning handle turnscrews,
Thro' ages folk made to retreat.

Quaint, olde-worlde thatched cottages,
Patterned in individual style
Aged rights-of-way, brook footbridges,
Milestones, turnstiles and stepping stiles.

No other land likens UK,
When Brits wet their feet overseas,
After a time yearn British life's way
And unbeatable cup of tea.

History shows how tyrants sink,
Thirsting British soil and tea to drink.

Hilary Jill Robson

KERNOW
(Kernow is Cornish for Cornwall)

'Cornwall is the last county in England.'
'I beg your pardon?'
'Cornwall is the last county in England.'
'Excuse me . . .'
'Are you deaf? I said . . .'
'I know what you *said*. Listen to me, ol' dear,
Cornwall is *not* a county. Cornwall is a country.
Understand, do 'ee? We be Cornish, we bain't English.
You do come from they Angles and Saxons, Vikings an' such-like.
We do come from Celtic roots, Christian long before
Augustine came from Rome to convert the Sawsnek.
We do have our own language, same root as Welsh.
Last spoken 1777 by Dolly Pentreath; still here today.
We do have our own thin places all around us,
Mystery and mystic, past, present and future.
When our mines was workin', you could hear the knockers.
No man must whistle in the mines. Bad luck.
Some do say the knockers be Pharisees, cast out
For condemning Christ. Treat 'em with respect.
And we always leave a piece o'crowst* be'ind,
Keep the piskies kind to us. As for food -
Your up-country pasties bain't pasties at all.
Pasties be a full meal. Last 'ee the day, they will.
Then there's saffron cake, an' heavy cake an'
Cornish cream, more than your Devon clotted.
An' starry-gazey pie* . . .

Laws? We do have our Stannary Laws. We know
To fight for freedom, of religion, of taxation.
Have you not heard the Cornish choirs 'And shall Trelawney die'?
Oh, my dear, 'ee do 'ave some lot to learn 'bout us.

*crowst = elevenses
* starry-gazey pie = with heads of pilchards sticking out of the pastry.

Elizabeth Morris

SUMMERTIME SPLENDOUR

Summertime splendour
is here at last . . .
Winter and Spring
have all just passed . . .
Afternoon heat . . .
is the talk of the days . . .
Lemonade cools
the sun's hot rays . . .

Summertime splendour
won't be here for long . . .
Be sure you enjoy
all the Summer birdsong . . .
Summer's a season
lazy days, out in the air . . .
Picking all the berries,
and going to the fair . . .

Summertime splendour
makes my heart want to sing . . .
Making summertime memories . . .
for remembering . . .

Carol Olson

MONARCHS AND PRINCES OF THE THIRD MILLENNIUM

A thousand years has time devoured,
ten centuries of life and death.
Each day on day the Earth spun round,
each night sleep claimed with stealth.

Monarchs and princes power did hold,
the Kingdom of Earth was theirs.
Lust and greed became the way
and passed to newborn heirs.

Yet, silently, God's unseen hand
with love the Heavens obeyed.
His unknown fate for human souls
by no force could be swayed.

With dimming minds we look behind
at years beyond our reach.
Our globe goes round no faster still,
life's waves pound up the beach.

The millennium now we all do face
is full of hopes and fears,
but seekers of power should ever dread
the next one thousand years.

E G Pryor

2001!

The year 2001 sees the end of the Dome,
It also starts with plenty of gloom,
What to do to turn this world around,
For happiness to grow instead of frowns,
World population exploding,
Further ecological corrosion,
Nature doing its best,
To cause atmospheric unrest.
Flood disruption to livelihood,
Sea causing landslides, not good,
What to do to turn this world around,
For happiness to grow instead of frowns,
To blame ourselves is a must,
Attention to materialistic lives, a lust,
Ease the load with more trust,
And stave off politicians rust.

Barbara R Lockwood

On Reflection

The Millennium we welcomed
With eager accolade
Sweeps swiftly along
On the crest of a wave
Are we rocking the boat
In the new Century rave?

Prosperity assured
We embraced the new dawn
Of automated confusion
Concede and conform
Our destiny determined
By screen, button and reform.

Past glories submit
To change and rearrange
Yet history may prove
In some future review
That this did not better
The traditional we knew.

Jack Pritchard

THIRD WORLD COUNTRY

We walked towards Oldbury's Council building
People, frustrated, sweaty, communities, creeds mingling
E09 my number, Rebecca keeps one company
Standing among well-dressed, the scruffy and frumpy
Old, smelly men, noisy children, the edgy, the jumpy
One of the security guards brought me a chair
We couldn't sit down, too many people were there
I'd completed my forms of endless questions
We sat waiting contemplating Council's objections
An old lady tottered on her walking frame
Black and white, young, old, the capable, the lame
Massing unsatisfied customers, cogitating, debating
And after two hours, we're all still waiting
No 97 she shouts, because the thingamajig's broken
Shoving his way through, this overweight bloke's suddenly spoken.
He raises his voice and waves papers in the air
'This is a bloody, lousy country, these rates are unfair.'
'Blame Maggie Thatcher,' someone shouts aloud
Sending oo's and aa's through the waiting crowd.
Number E09, Booth Seven, 'Thank God for that.'
Pushing my forms under her reinforced hatch
Stony-faced, old crow, she flicks through pages
She doesn't care that we've waited ages.
'Are you selling your property?'
'No,' firmly I shout
'Well, you've filled in that section.' Scowling she crosses it out.
It took her five minutes to process my claim
And come next June, I'll have to bloody wait there again.

Ann Hathaway

THE MILLENNIUM FOR THE PEOPLE

A new millennium or so we are told,
It's time to face the future, new truths to unfold,
So far nothing has changed, things have stayed the same,
New commitments, new choices, it drives you insane.

It has no meaning for me or for you,
Time is passing quickly, the words are but for a few,
So many struggling, just trying to get by,
The goals have been set, may as well reach for the sky.

A light in the distance, could show the way,
No more taxation, something to remember, something to say,
More help for the people, the suffering and the old,
More caring and loving, understanding, come out of the cold.

New life, new beginnings, words that have meaning,
No more empty promises, to the 21st century we are leaning.
Children's faces smiling, enough food for the world,
Learn from the mistakes, the last century hurled.

Dianne Brown

LOOKING ON

Above in the blue sky you rest your head,
Looking down upon this world that surrounds me.
You visit me so very much, helping me along the way,
Shining all the good luck you can down on me.
As I look up to the stars they frame your face,
Your voice is carried from one end to another for me.
I feel you close if I am insure or in need,
You are my second body, heart and mind.
The words you taught stay afloat, always alive,
My life takes the same path as yours once did.
I say the way I feel, I see you, always ready to listen,
Even though we are worlds apart you seem so near.
My hand reaches out as it did years ago,
The warmth I feel brings back the fondest memories.
You and me will forever have this tie between us,
I only glimpse up above to see you are here.

Zoe Fitzjohn

GATE OF LIFE

I opened up this gate of life
Looked back on its many miles,
Times of sorrow of haunted memories
My heartache, tears and strife.
In the warmth of the summer's heat
On this path of life
I cross many a stile of green meadows,
Babbling brooks where woods stand in file.
Gently the summer rain falls at my feet,
Across green pastures of calling rooks
I wait awhile.
My history now written in my book
I close this gate of life,
Looking out towards the hills
The summer wind, blows a kiss on me.
Across a new season another land
Beyond the sorrow that I weep,
A tractor cuts its furrows
Of many a rift of grief.
I stumble, trip, fall over steps I miss
To a new path, a new life
A new gate I greet.

Frederick Fordham

A Peaceful Time

She climbed over the gate and through the field
she strolled, the evening breeze gently blowing
her long, dark hair, the heat from the sun
warmed her tanned skin.

Her day had been one of frustration
nothing had gone right at all
problems created by others
she had been at everyone's beck and call.

Walking here she felt at peace,
relieved of inner tension,
church bells rang out in the air
she smiled with satisfaction.

Beyond the trees a winding stream
that seemed to stretch for miles,
she took off her shoes and bathed her feet
then rested for a while.

The chiming of the church clock
told her it was getting late,
so she retraced her steps across the field
disappearing over the gate.

Linda Beavis

Remembering

Across a forlorn field of corn,
That once soldiers fought and won.
A lonely soul stands to recall,
The place where he had lost a son.
So here I am in Normandy so green,
To where my brother had been cut down,
By that same cornfield, so peaceful now,
So near a little Bogage town.
But my poor brother, wounded and near the end,
Had battled to make it home again,
And so he did with help from many,
As on the way they did their best to ease his pain.
For him to live out his life with those who cared,
With who, in turn, each day he gladly shared.

Elisabeth Dill Perrin

DAYSTAR

Golden radiance sparkles
coating Earth with glittering threads
invisible fingers of healing warmth
penetrate the cold flesh below

Life stirs and raises its head
revelling in the precious beams
reaching out to grasp the silent moments
hungrily savouring life-giving heat

Eye of Heaven gazes below with benign fervour
blazing Mother spreads her arms, embraces infinity
sheds her dazzling flame for mortals, her source their survival
flaming lashes moist sighting elation her gift creates

Glow of Phoebus bathes the sea
sparkling silver mirror reflects coruscant rays
liquid movement spangles lustrous jewel
rippling fingers cast high the scintilla, illume cyanic depths

Sandra Bond

SUBMISSIONS INVITED
SOMETHING FOR EVERYONE

POETRY NOW 2001 - Any subject, any style, any time.

WOMENSWORDS 2001 - Strictly women, have your say the female way!

STRONGWORDS 2001 - Warning! Age restriction, must be between 16-24, opinionated and have strong views. (Not for the faint-hearted)

All poems no longer than 30 lines.
Always welcome! No fee!
Cash Prizes to be won!

Mark your envelope (eg *Poetry Now*) **2001**
Send to:
Forward Press Ltd
Remus House, Coltsfoot Drive,
Peterborough, PE2 9JX

OVER £10,000 POETRY PRIZES TO BE WON!

Judging will take place in October 2001